The *Titanic* Reports

The Official Conclusions of the 1912 Inquiries Into the *Titanic* Disaster by the US Senate and the British Wreck Commissioner

Red and Black Publishers, St Petersburg, Florida

Report Of The Committee On Commerce United States Senate Pursuant To S. Res. 283 Directing The Committee On Commerce To Investigate The Causes Leading To The Wreck Of The White Star Liner *Titanic*. Originally published 1912

British Wreck Commissioner's Inquiry Report on the Loss of the *Titanic*. Command Paper of the House of Commons Cd6392, 1912-1913 session. Originally published 1912

Library of Congress Cataloging-in-Publication Data

The Titanic reports : the official conclusions of the 1912 inquiries
 into the Titanic disaster / by the US Senate and the British Wreck
 Commissioner.
        p. cm.
    ISBN 978-1-934941-11-9
  1. Titanic (Steamship)--Sources. 2. Shipwrecks--North Atlantic
Ocean--Sources. I. United States. Congress. Senate. Committee on Commerce.
"Titanic" disaster II. Great Britain. Court to investigate loss of
steamship "Titanic". Proceedings before the Right Hon. Lord Mersey, wreck
commissioner of the United Kingdom ...
    VK1255.T6T58 2008
    910.9163'4--dc22

                                                            2008009879

Red and Black Publishers, PO Box 7542, St Petersburg, Florida, 33734
Contact us at: info@RedandBlackPublishers.com

Printed and manufactured in the United States of America

Preface

The American Congressional inquiry into the sinking of the *Titanic*, in April 1912, very nearly did not take place – and the reasons were legal and economic.

When the world learned, on the morning of April 15, 1912, that the *Titanic* had struck an iceberg and sunk, Michigan Senator William Alden Smith paid particular attention to the press reports. Senator Smith had previously met the *Titanic's* captain, William J. Smith (no relation) on another vessel, during a trans-Atlantic trip in 1906. By late afternoon, Senator Smith became more and more disturbed by the details he was seeing in the press reports – not enough lifeboats for all the passengers, the *Titanic* perhaps ignoring ice warnings and traveling at excessive speed. The White Star Line that owned the *Titanic*, Senator Smith knew, was itself a part of the International Mercantile Marine Company (IMM), an American holding company that was incorporated in New Jersey and financed by the American banker J. Pierpont Morgan. In addition, the *Titanic* had been traveling to an American port, and most of its passengers were immigrants who were about to become American citizens. Convinced that the US government had an interest in finding out exactly what had happened, Senator Smith telephoned the White House to ask what President Theodore Roosevelt planned to do regarding the accident, and was told by Roosevelt's secretary that the President intended to let the British Board of Trade handle any investigation.

On April 17, however, after it became apparent that the only survivors had already been picked up by the British liner *Carpathia*, and that the loss of life on the *Titanic* had been heavy, Senator Smith introduced a resolution calling for an investigation into the accident by a subcommittee of the Senate's Commerce Committee. Smith was named Chairman, and six other Senators – three Republicans and three Democrats – were chosen to serve on the subcommittee.

The next day, the newly-formed panel received word that critically endangered their investigation even before it had begun. The US Navy informed Senator Smith that it had intercepted a message to the White Star office in New York from someone aboard the *Carpathia*. The cable read:

> Most desirable *Titanic* crew aboard *Carpathia* should be returned home earliest moment possible. Suggest you hold *Cedric*, sailing her daylight Friday unless you see any reason contrary. Propose returning in her myself.
>
> YAMSI

It didn't take a Navy codebreaker to know that "YAMSI" was J. Bruce Ismay, the Chairman of IMM who had been on board the *Titanic*, and was now approaching the United States, with the rest of the survivors, aboard the *Carpathia*. To Senator Smith, it looked suspiciously as if Ismay wanted to quickly spirit himself and all his employees back to England without even setting foot in America, thereby denying any reporters (or investigators) the opportunity to question any of the crew, and placing everyone out of reach of subpoenas for any potential American court hearing (Ismay didn't yet know that the US Senate had already formed its own investigation of the disaster).

For anyone who was familiar with American maritime law, the reason for Ismay's anxious desire to avoid any questioning by United States authorities was obvious, and it came down to one word: liability.

In the early days of trans-Atlantic travel, sailing between America and Europe was risky—the North Atlantic was stormy, unpredictable and dangerous. In order to lessen the financial risk and to encourage trans-Atlantic shipping, the US adopted, in 1851, a doctrine of maritime law known as "limitation of liability". In effect, this provision removed most of the liability on the part of a ship-owner for any action over which it had no direct control, including the negligent actions of a ship's captain or crew at sea. In such circumstances, the owner of the ship was limited in liability to only the value of any cargo lost.

There was, however, an exception to the limited liability doctrine—and it applied directly to the *Titanic* disaster. The ship-owner's liability was no longer limited if that owner had been in contact with the ship's commander during a voyage and had in any way directed or controlled the actions undertaken by the ship's captain while the ship was at sea.

Ismay, the President of IMM and the Chairman of the White Star Line which owned the *Titanic*, was not merely in wireless contact with the captain during the voyage, however—he was actually aboard the ship. Ismay's reputation was already in tatters, since it was widely believed by the American public that he had used his influence as the ship's owner to obtain a seat in a lifeboat, and thus to save his own life at the expense of the passengers. Ismay's presence on the ship, however, as both he and Senator Smith realized, presented a far greater threat to him than merely a reputation as a coward. If it could be shown that Ismay had exercised any influence over the actions of *Titanic's* Captain Smith - in setting the ship's course and speed in order to make a timely passage, for example—then IMM and White Star, as the *Titanic's* owners, would no longer be protected by the "limited liability" doctrine, and could be sued in American courts by all of the 700 survivors and all 1,500 victims' next of kin. Ismay, White Star and IMM all faced potential bankruptcy if a US court denied them the limited liability protection.

For Senator Smith, the news that Ismay wanted to leave the US immediately (and take his British crew with him) raised suspicions that, between the lack of lifeboats and the potential for full liability, the owners of the *Titanic* had something to hide. By noon that day, Smith was at the White House asking the Attorney General whether the US had the legal right to subpoena Ismay and the *Titanic* crew, who were all British citizens. Upon being informed that the Englishmen could be legally served with a subpoena as long as they were in the US, Smith met with the rest of the Senate subcommittee and, accompanied by Senator Francis Newlands, boarded a train for

New York. Immediately upon arrival, the two Senators served a total of 20 subpoenas upon Ismay and the *Titanic* officers and crew, requiring them to appear at hearings that were hastily scheduled for the next morning, April 19, at the New York Waldorf-Astoria.

The British inquiry was started on April 22, when the President of the British Board of Trade appointed Charles Bigham, Lord Mersey, to serve as Chairman of the Wreck Commission. The hearings began on May 2, 1912.

US Senate

Report Of The Committee To Investigate The Causes Leading To The Wreck Of The White Star Liner *Titanic*.

Mr. SMITH of Michigan, from the Committee on Commerce, submitted the following:

REPORT.

(Pursuant to S. Res. 283.)

The Committee on Commerce, which was authorized and directed to inquire into the loss of the British steamship *Titanic*, respectfully reports that that duty has been performed, and the committee has reached its conclusions thereon.

The resolution is as follows:

Resolved, that the Committee on Commerce, or a subcommittee thereof, is hereby authorized and directed to investigate the causes leading to the wreck of the White Star liner *Titanic*, with its attendant loss of life so shocking to the civilized world.

Resolved further, that said committee or a subcommittee thereof is hereby empowered to summon witnesses, send for persons and papers, to administer oaths, and take such testimony as may be necessary to determine the responsibility therefore, with a view to such legislation as may be necessary to prevent, as far as possible, any repetition of such a disaster.

Resolved further, that the committee shall inquire particularly into the number of lifeboats, life rafts, and life preservers, and other equipment for the protection of the passengers and crew; the number of persons aboard the *Titanic*, whether passenger or crew, and whether adequate inspections were made of such vessel, in view of the large number of American passengers traveling over a route commonly regarded as dangerous from icebergs; and whether it is feasible for Congress to take steps looking to an international agreement to secure the protection of sea traffic, including regulation of the size of ships and designation of routes.

Resolved further, that in the report of said committee it shall recommend such legislation as it shall deem expedient; and the expenses incurred by this investigation shall be paid from the contingent fund of the Senate upon vouchers to be approved by the chairman of said Committee.

Attest,

CHARLES G. BENNETT, Secretary.

By H. M. ROSE, Assistant Secretary.

Accordingly the following Senators were pointed his members of the subcommittee: William Alden Smith, Michigan, chairman; George C. Perkins, California; Jonathan Bourne, Jr., Oregon; Theodore E. Burton, Ohio; F. M. Simmons, North Carolina; Francis G. Newlands, Nevada; Duncan U. Fletcher, Florida.

WITNESSES EXAMINED.

We examined 82 witnesses upon various phases of this catastrophe, including the examination of 53 British subjects or residents of Great Britain and 29 citizens of United States or residents thereof.

We interrogated two general officers of the International Mercantile Marine Co., which owned the steamship *Titanic* - J. Bruce Ismay, of Liverpool, England, president, also a passenger on the ship on this voyage, and P. A. S. Franklin, of New York, vice president in the United States of the International Mercantile Marine Co.; all the surviving officers, 4 in number - Charles Herbert Lightoller, Second Officer, of Netley Abbey, Hampshire, England; Third Officer Herbert John Pitman, of Somerset, England; Fourth Officer Joseph Grove Boxhall, of Hull, England; and Fifth Officer Harold Godfrey Lowe, of North Wales; and 34 members of the crew, whose names are as follows:

Andrews, C. E.	Assistant Steward	145 Millbrook Road, Southampton
Archer, Ernest	Seaman	59 Porchester Road, Southampton.
Barrett, Frederick	Leading Fireman	Southampton
Brice, W.	Seaman	11 Lower Canal Walk, Southampton.
Bride, H. S.	Telegrapher	London, England.
Bright, A. J.	Quartermaster	105 Firgrove Road, Southampton.
Buley, E. J.	Seaman	10 Cliff Road, Woolston, Southampton.
Burke, W.	Saloon Steward	57 Bridge Road, Southampton.
Clench, F.	Seaman	10 The Flats Chantry Road, Southampton.
Collins, J.	Assistant Cook	65 Ballycarry, Belfast.
Crawford, A.	Bedroom Steward	22 Cranbury Avenue, Southampton.
Crowe, G. F.	Steward	89 Milton Road, Southampton.
Cunningham, A.	Bedroom Steward	62 Charlton Road, Southampton.
Etches, H. S.	Bedroom Steward	23a Gordon Avenue, Southampton.
Evans, F. O.	Seaman	14 Bond Street, Southampton.
Fleet, F.	Lookout (sailor)	No. 9 Norman Road, Southampton.
Haines, Albert	Boatswain's Mate	No. 52 Groves Street, Southampton.
Hardy, J.	Steward	Oakley Holyrood Avenue, Highfield, Southampton.
Hemming, Samuel S.	Lamp Trimmer	31 Kingsley Road, Southampton.
Hichens, Robert	Quartermaster	43 James Street, Southampton.
Hogg, G. A.	Lookout (sailor)	44 High Street, Southampton.
Jones, Thomas	Seaman	68 Wesfield, Liverpool.
Moore, G.	Seaman	51 Graham Avenue, Southampton.
Olliver, A.	Quartermaster	38 Anderson Road, Southampton.
Osman, F.	Seaman	43 High Street, Itchen, Southampton.
Perkis, W. A.	Quartermaster	Victoria Road, Bitterne, Southampton.

Ray, F. D.	Saloon Steward	Palmer Park Avenue, Reading.
Rowe, G. T.	Quartermaster	63 Henry Street, Gosport.
Symons, G.	Lookout (sailor)	55 Franchise Street, Weymouth.
Taylor, W. H.	Fireman	No. 2 Broad Street, Southampton.
Ward, W.	Saloon Steward	Norwood House, Shireley, Southampton.
Weikman, A. H.	Barber	9 Dyer Road, Ivybank.
Wheelton, E.	Steward	Norwood House, Shirley, Southampton.
Widgery, J.	Bath Steward	25 Rokeby Avenue, Redland, Bristol.

We took the testimony of 21 passengers of all classes (including President Ismay) and 23 other witnesses on subjects related to our inquiry (including vice president Franklin).

We held our sessions in New York and in Washington, and took testimony by deposition in other parts of the country and in the Dominion of Canada.

The results of our investigation may be stated as follows:

OWNERSHIP OF STEAMSHIP *TITANIC*.

We find that the *Titanic* was a White Star steamer and was owned by the Oceanic Steam Navigation Co., of England, all of the stock of which company is in turn owned by the International Navigation Co. (Ltd.), of England, and the stock of that company, in turn, is owned by the International Mercantile Marine Co., an American corporation, organized under the laws of New Jersey.

INTERNATIONAL MERCANTILE MARINE CO.

Mr. J. Bruce Ismay, of Liverpool, England, is president of the International Mercantile Marine Co., and Mr. P. A. S. Franklin, of New York City, is vice president of that company in United States.

The Board of Directors of the International Mercantile Marine Co. is composed of the following persons:

C. A. Griscom, Chairman. E. C. Grenfell. John F. Archbold. John I. Waterbury. The Right Hon. Lord Pirrie George W. Perkins. Charles Steele. J. Bruce Ismay, President. Percy Chubb. E. J. Berwind. Harold A. Sanderson. P. A. B. Widener. Charles F. Torrey. J. P. Morgan, Jr.

The International Mercantile Marine Co., through its various ramifications and constituent companies, owns the White Star Line, the American Line, the Red Star Line, the Atlantic Transport Line, the National Line, and the majority of the stock of the Leyland Line.

This company is capitalized as follows (in round numbers):

$102,000,000 between preferred and common shares.$ 52,000,000 of 4 1/2 percent bonds.$ 19,000,000 (about) of 5 percent bonds.$ 7,000,000 (about) of underlying bonds.

The total stock and bonded liability is about $180,000,000.

This company owns and operates a fleet of about 125 vessels, with a total of about 1,150,000 tons register, doing a general transoceanic transportation business throughout the world.

Titanic

GENERAL PARTICULARS OF STEAMSHIP *TITANIC*.

The *Titanic* was built by Harland and Wolff, of Belfast, Ireland. No restriction as to limit of cost was placed upon the builders. She was launched May 31, 1911. She was a vessel of 46,328 tons register; her length was 882.6 feet, and her breadth was 92.6 feet. Her boat deck and bridge were 70 feet above the waterline. She was, according to the testimony of President Ismay, "especially constructed to float with her two largest watertight compartments full of water."

The vessel, fully equipped, cost £1,500,000 sterling, or about $7,500,000.

At the time of the accident the vessel carried insurance of £1,000,000 sterling or about $5,000,000, the remaining risk being carried by the company's insurance fund.

The *Titanic* was a duplicate of the *Olympic*, which is owned by the same company, with a single exception of her passenger accommodations, and was built to accommodate 2,599 passengers, with additional accommodations for officers and crew numbering 903 persons.

TRIAL TESTS STEAMSHIP *TITANIC*.

The committee finds from the evidence that between six and seven hours was spent in making trial tests of this vessel at Belfast Lough on Monday, the 1st of April last. A few turning circles were made, compasses adjusted, and she steamed a short time under approximately a full head of steam, but the ship was not driven at her full speed. One general officer of the steamship company was on board during the trial tests, while the builders were represented by Mr. Thomas Andrews, who had superintended the building of the vessel. Mr. Andrews conducted certain tests at Southampton and represented the builders both at Southampton and on the first voyage.

With a partial crew, the ship sailed from Belfast, immediately after the trial, for Southampton, where she arrived on Wednesday, April 3, about midnight. She made fast with her port side to the wharf, where she remained until April 10, about 12 o'clock noon, when she sailed for Cherbourg, Queenstown, and New York.

ONLY TWO LIFEBOATS LOWERED.

Many of the crew did not join the ship until a few hours before sailing, and the only drill while the vessel lay at Southampton or on the voyage consisted in lowering two lifeboats on the starboard side into the water, which boats were again hoisted to the boat deck within a half hour. No boat list designating the stations of members of the crew was posted until several days after sailing from Southampton, boatmen being left in ignorance of their proper stations until the following Friday morning.

CERTIFICATE OF BRITISH BOARD OF TRADE.

On Wednesday morning, the day the ship sailed from Southampton, Capt. Clark, a representative of the British Board of Trade, came aboard and, after spending a brief time, issued the necessary certificate to permit sailing.

BOAT DAVITS AND LIFEBOATS OF THE STEAMSHIP *TITANIC*.

The *Titanic* was fitted with 16 sets of double-acting boat davits of modern type, capable of handling 2 or 3 boats per set of davits. The davits were thus capable of handling 48 boats, whereas the ship carried but 16 lifeboats and 4 collapsibles, fulfilling all the requirements of the British Board of Trade. The *Titanic* was provided with 14 lifeboats, of capacity for 65 persons each, or 910 persons; 2 emergency sea boats, of capacity for 35 persons each, or 70 persons; 4 collapsible boats, of capacity for 49 persons each, or 196 persons. Total lifeboat capacity, 1,176. There was ample lifebelt equipment for all.

DEPARTURE OF THE STEAMSHIP *TITANIC*.

The ship left Southampton Wednesday, April 10, at 12.15 p.m., with the ship's complement of officers and crew numbering 899 persons. As the *Titanic* left the wharf at Southampton the moorings of the *New York* were carried away by the backwash from the *Titanic*'s starboard propeller, causing a delay of about half an hour.

PASSENGER LIST AND SURVIVORS OF STEAMSHIP *TITANIC*.

The *Titanic* arrived at Cherbourg late the same afternoon. The *Titanic* left Cherbourg and proceeded to Queenstown, Ireland, arriving there on Thursday about midday, departing for New York immediately after embarking the mails and passengers. Her passenger list was made up as follows:

first class passengers who sailed on the *Titanic*:
Women and Children   156   Men   173   Total   329
first class passengers, survivors:
Women and Children   145   Men   54   Total   199
first class passengers, lost:
Women and Children   11   Men   119   Total   130
second class passengers who sailed on the *Titanic*:
Women and Children   128   Men   157   Total   285
second class passengers, survivors:
Women and Children   104   Men   15   Total   119
second class passengers, lost:

Women and Children   24   Men   142   Total   166

third class passengers who sailed on the *Titanic*:

Women and Children   224   Men   486   Total   710

third class passengers, survivors:

Women and Children   105   Men   69   Total   174

third class passengers, lost:

Women and Children   119   Men   417   Total   536

SUMMARY OF PASSENGERS AND SURVIVORS.

	On Board		
	Women/Children	Men	Total
First Class	156	173	329
Second Class	128	157	285
Third Class	224	476	710
Total Passengers	508	816	1,324
Crew	23	876	899
Total	531	1,692	2,223

	Saved		
	Women/Children	Men	Total
First Class	145	54	199
Second Class	104	15	119
Third Class	105	69	174
Total Passengers	354	138	492
Crew	20	194	214
Total	374	332	706

	Lost			
	Women/Children	Men	Total	Percent Saved
First Class	11	119	130	60
Second Class	24	142	166	42
Third Class	119	417	536	25
Total Passengers	154	678	832	.....
Crew	3	682	685	24
Total	157	1,360	1,517	32

Voyage

WEATHER CONDITIONS DURING VOYAGE.

During the entire voyage the weather was clear, with the single exception of 10 minutes of fog, and the sea was calm throughout the voyage, with sunshine the whole of each day and bright starlight every night. No untoward incident marred the trip. Greetings were frequently exchanged with passing vessels by appropriate signals.

ICE WARNINGS.

On the third day out ice warnings were received by the wireless operators on the *Titanic*, and the testimony is conclusive that at least three of these warnings came direct to the commander of the *Titanic* on the day the accident, the first about noon, from the *Baltic*, of the White Star Line. It will be noted that this message places icebergs within five miles of the track which the *Titanic* was following, and near the place were the accident occurred. The message from the commander of the *Baltic* is as follows (p. 1061):

> STEAMSHIP *BALTIC*, April 14, 1912.
>
> Capt. SMITH, *Titanic*:
>
> Have had moderate variable winds and clear fine weather since leaving. Greek steamer *Athinai* reports passing icebergs and large quantity of field ice today in latitude 41.51 north, longitude 49.52 west. Last night we spoke German oil tank *Deutschland*, *Stettin* to Philadelphia, not under control; short of coal; latitude 40.42 north, longitude 55.11. Wishes to be reported to New York and other steamers. Wish you and *Titanic* all success.
>
> COMMANDER.

The second message was received by the *Titanic* from the *Californian*, of the Leyland line, at 5.35 p.m. New York time, Sunday afternoon, reporting ice about 19 miles to the northward of the track which the *Titanic* was following. This message was as follows (p. 735):

> Latitude 42.3 north, longitude 49.9 west. Three large bergs 5 miles to southward of us. Regards.
>
> (Sig.) Lord.

The third message was transmitted from the *Amerika* via the *Titanic* and Cape Race to the Hydrographic Office in Washington, D.C., reporting ice about 19 miles to the southward of the course being followed by the *Titanic*, and reads as follows (p. 507):

> STEAMSHIP *AMERIKA*, VIA *Titanic* and Cape Race, N. F.
>
> HYDROGRAPHIC OFFICE, Washington D.C.:
>
> *Amerika* past two large icebergs and 41.27 N., 50.8 W., on the 14th of April
>
> K. N. U. T.

This message was actually received at the Hydrographic Office in Washington at 10.51 p.m., April 14.

The fourth message was sent to the *Titanic* at 9.05 p.m. New York time, on Sunday, the 14th of April, approximately an hour before the accident occurred. The message reads as follows:

> We are stopped and surrounded by ice.

To this the operator of the *Titanic* replied:

> Shut up. I am busy. I am working Cape Race.

While this was the last message sent by the *Californian* to the *Titanic*, the evidence shows that the operator of the *Californian* kept the telephones on his head, and heard the *Titanic* talking to Cape Race up to within a few minutes of the time of the accident, when he "put the phones down, took off his clothes, and turned in."

The *Baltic*'s operator on that Sunday overheard ice reports going to the *Titanic* from the *Prinz Friedrich Wilhelm*, and from the *Amerika* (p. 1061), while the *Carpathia* on the same day overheard the *Parisian* talking about ice with other ships (p. 497).

ICE BOTH TO NORTHWARD AND SOUTHWARD OF STEAMSHIP *TITANIC*'S TRACK.

This enables the committee to say that the ice positions so definitely reported to the *Titanic* just preceding the accident located ice on both sides of the track or lane which the *Titanic* was following, and in her immediate vicinity. No general discussion took place among the officers; no conference was called to consider these warnings; no heed was given to them. The speed was not relaxed, the lookout was not increased, and the only vigilance displayed by the officer of the watch was by instructions to the lookouts to keep "a sharp lookout for ice." It should be said, however, that the testimony shows that Capt. Smith remarked to Officer Lightoller, who was the officer doing duty on the bridge until 10 o'clock ship's time, or 8.27 o'clock New York time, "If it was in a slight degree hazy there would be no doubt we should have to go very slowly" (p. 67), and "If in the slightest degree doubtful, let me know." The evidence is that it was exceptionally clear. There was no haze, and the ship's speed was not reduced.

SPEED.

The speed of the *Titanic* was gradually increased after leaving Queenstown. The first day's run was 464 miles, the second day's run was 519 miles, the third day's run was 546 miles. Just prior to the collision the ship was making her maximum speed of the voyage - not less than 21 knots, or 24 1/4 miles per hour.

Collision

THE COLLISION.

At 11.46 p.m. ship's time, or 10.13 p.m. New York time, Sunday evening, April 14, the lookout signaled the bridge and telephoned the Officer of the watch, "Iceberg right ahead." The Officer of the watch, Mr. Murdoch, immediately ordered the Quartermaster at the wheel to put the helm "hard astarboard," and reversed the engines; but while the Sixth Officer standing behind the Quartermaster at the wheel reported to Officer Murdoch "The helm is hard astarboard," the *Titanic* stuck the ice (pp. 229 and 450). The impact, while not violent enough to disturb the passengers or crew, or to arrest the ship's progress, rolled the vessel slightly and tore the steel plating above the turn of the bilge.

FIRST DAMAGE REPORTED.

The testimony shows that coincident with the collision air was heard whistling or hissing from the overflow pipe to the forepeak tank, indicating the escape of air from that tank because of the inrush of water. Practically at once, the forepeak tank, No. 1 hold, No. 2 hold, No. 3 hold, and forward boiler room, filled with water, the presence of which was immediately reported from the mail room and the racquet court and trunk room in No. 3 hold, and also from the firemen's quarters in No. 1 hold. Leading Fireman Barrett saw the water rushing into the forward fireroom from a tear about two feet above the stokehold floor plates and about twenty feet below the waterline, which tear extended two feet into the coal bunker at the forward end of the second fireroom.

SERIOUS NATURE OF DAMAGE REALIZED.

The reports received by the Captain after various inspections of the ship must have acquainted him promptly with its serious condition, and when interrogated by President Ismay, he so expressed himself. It is believed, also, that this serious condition was promptly realized by the chief engineer and by the builders' representative, Mr. Andrews, none of whom survived.

FLOODING OF THE VESSEL.

Under this added weight of water the bow of the ship sank deeper and deeper into the water, and through the open hatch leading from the mail room, and through other openings, water promptly overflowed E deck, below which deck the third, fourth, fifth, sixth, seventh, and eighth transverse bulkheads ended, and thus flooded the compartments abaft No. 3 hold.

WATERTIGHT COMPARTMENTS.

The *Titanic* was fitted with 15 transverse watertight bulkheads, only 1, the first bulkhead from forward, extended to the uppermost continuous deck, C; bulkheads Nos. 2, 10, 11, 12, 13, 14, and 15 extended to the second continuous deck, D; and bulkheads Nos. 3, 4, 5, 6, 7, 8, and 9 extended only to the third continuous deck, E. The openings through deck E were not designed for watertight closing, as the evidence shows that flooding over deck E contributed largely to the sinking of vessel. The bulkheads above described divided the ship into 16 main watertight compartments, and the ship was so arranged that any 2 main compartments might be flooded without in any way involving the safety of the ship. As before stated, the testimony shows that the 5 extreme forward compartments were flooded practically immediately, and under such circumstances, by reason of the non watertight character of the deck at which the transverse bulkheads ended, the supposedly watertight compartments were *not* watertight, and the sinking of the vessel followed.

DISTRESS CALLS SENT OUT.

No general alarm was sounded, no whistle blown, and no systematic warning was given the passengers. Within 15 or 20 minutes the Captain visited the wireless room and instructed the operator to get assistance, sending out the distress call, C.Q.D.

Pleas For Help

DISTRESS CALLS HEARD.

This distress call was heard by the wireless station at Cape Race that evening at 10.25 p.m. New York time, together with the report that she had struck an iceberg, and at the same time was accidentally overheard by the *Mount Temple*, which ship was immediately turned around (p. 760) toward the *Titanic*. Within two or three minutes a reply was received from the *Frankfurt*. Within ten minutes the wireless operator of the *Carpathia* fortunately and largely by chance heard the *Titanic*'s C.Q.D. call (pp. 901 and 929), which he reported at once to the bridge and to the Captain. The *Carpathia* was immediately turned around (p. 19) and reported her latitude and longitude to the *Titanic*, together with the fact that she was steaming full speed toward the stricken ship (pp. 148 and 901). The *Frankfurt*, however, did not give her latitude or longitude, and after waiting 20 minutes asked the operator of the *Titanic*, "What is the matter?" To this the *Titanic* replied that he was a fool (pp. 151 and 153).

In view of the fact that no position had been given by the *Frankfurt*, and that her exact distance from the *Titanic* was unknown at that time, the answer of the operator of the *Titanic* was scarcely such as prudence would have dictated. Notwithstanding this, however, the *Frankfurt* was overheard by the *Mount Temple* to report "Our captain will go for you" (p. 929). Communication was promptly established with the *Olympic* and the *Baltic* (pp. 151, 158, and 901), and the *Coronia*, some 800 miles to the eastward, overheard the *Titanic's* C.Q.D. call. The wireless messages of the *Titanic* were recorded in part by the Cape Race station (p. 175) and by the *Mount Temple* (p. 929), and in part by the *Baltic* (pp. 1059 and 1060). The *Mount Temple* last heard the *Titanic* after the accident at 11.47 p.m. New York time (p. 929). The *Baltic* and the *Carpathia* lost touch about the same time, the last message they received being "Engine room getting flooded" (pp. 107 and 1062). The *Virginian* last heard the *Titanic's* signals at 12.27 New York time, and reported them blurred, and ending abruptly (p. 175).

FIRST PRESS REPORT.

This information is contained in a report received by the Associated Press from Cape Race, and communicated by them to the public, and also to Vice President Franklin of the White Star Line, and later verified from his office in Montreal, as follows (p. 1023):

CAPE RACE, NEW BRUNSWICK,

Sunday night, April 14.

At 10.25 o'clock to-night the White Star Line steamship *Titanic* called "C.Q.D." to the Marconi wireless station here and reported having struck an iceberg. The steamer said that immediate assistance was required.

Half an hour afterwards another message came, reporting that they were sinking by the head, and that women were being put off in the lifeboats.

The weather was calm and clear, the *Titanic*'s wireless operator reported, and gave the position of the vessel as 41.46 north latitude and 50.14 west longitude.

The Marconi station at Cape Race notified the Allan liner *Virginian*, the captain of which immediately advised that he was proceeding for the scene of the disaster.

The *Virginian* at midnight was about 170 miles distant from the *Titanic* and expected to reach that vessel about 10 a.m. Monday.

2 A.M. MONDAY.

The *Olympic* at an early hour this (Monday) morning was in latitude 40.32 north and longitude 61.18 west. She was in direct communication with the *Titanic* and is now making all haste toward her.

The steamship *Baltic* also reported herself as about 200 miles east of the *Titanic* and was making all possible speed toward her.

The last signals from the *Titanic* were heard by the *Virginian* at 12.27 a.m.

The wireless operator on the *Virginian* says these signals were blurred and ended abruptly.

VESSELS IN VICINITY OF STEAMSHIP *TITANIC*.

At this time the committee thinks it advisable to invite attention to the reported positions of the vessels in the vicinity of the *Titanic* when her calls of distress were being sent out.

The *Californian*, of the Leyland Line, west-bound, was in latitude 42° 05′ north, longitude 50° 07′ west, and was distant in a northerly direction 19 1/2 miles according to the Captain's figures (p. 717).

The *Mount Temple*, of the Canadian Pacific Railroad Line, west-bound, was in latitude 41° 25′ north, longitude 51° 14′ west, and was about 49 miles to the westward of the *Titanic* (pp. 759 and 760) and on her return to the *Titanic*'s position passed an unknown schooner.

The *Carpathia*, of the Cunard Line, east-bound, was 58 miles away, and she steered a course north 52° west to reach the *Titanic* (p. 20).

The *Birma*, a Russian ship, was 70 miles off at 12.25 a.m. on Monday, the 15th of April (pp. 780 and 929).

The *Frankfurt*, of the North German Lloyd Line, east-bound, was in latitude 39° 47′ north, longitude 52° 10′ west, 153 miles to the southwest (p. 772).

The *Virginian* at midnight was about 170 miles distant from the *Titanic* (p. 175).

The *Baltic*, of the White Star Line, east-bound, was about 243 miles southeast of the *Titanic*'s position at about 11 o'clock Sunday evening, New York time (p.1056).

The *Olympic*, of the White Star Line, east-bound, at 12.14, New York time, was about 512 miles to the westward, in latitude 40° 22′ north, longitude 61° 18′ west (p. 771).

STEAMSHIP LIGHT SEEN FROM STEAMSHIP *TITANIC*.

Sixteen witnesses from the *Titanic*, including officers and experienced seamen, and passengers of sound judgment, testified to seeing the light of a ship in the distance, and some of the lifeboats were directed to pull for that light, to leave the passengers and return to the side of the *Titanic*. The *Titanic* fired distress rockets and attempted to signal by electric lamp and Morse code to this vessel. At about the same time the officers of the *Californian* admit seeing rockets in the general direction of the *Titanic* and say that they immediately displayed a powerful Morse lamp, which could be easily seen a distance of 10 miles, while several of the crew the *Californian* testify that the side lights of a large vessel going at full speed were plainly visible from the lower deck of the *Californian* at 11.30 p.m., ship's time, just before the accident. There is no evidence that any rockets were fired by any vessel between the *Titanic* and the *Californian*, although every eye on the *Titanic* was searching the horizon for possible assistance.

STEAMSHIP *CALIFORNIAN*'S RESPONSIBILITY.

The committee is forced to the inevitable conclusion that the *Californian*, controlled by the same company, was nearer the *Titanic* than the 19 miles reported by her Captain, and that her officers and crew saw the distress signals of the *Titanic* and failed to respond to them in accordance with the dictates of humanity, international usage, and the requirements of law. The only reply to the distress signals was a counter signal from a large white light which was flashed for nearly two hours from the mast of the *Californian*. In our opinion such conduct, whether arising from indifference or gross carelessness, is most reprehensible, and places upon the commander the *Californian* a grave responsibility. The wireless operator of the *Californian* was not aroused until 3.30 a.m., New York time, on the morning of the 15th, after considerable conversation between officers and members of the crew had taken place aboard that ship regarding these distress signals or rockets, and was directed by the Chief Officer to see there was anything the matter, as a ship had been firing rockets during the night (p. 736). The inquiry thus set on foot immediately disclosed the fact that the *Titanic* had sunk. Had assistance been promptly proffered, or had the wireless operator of the *Californian* remained a few minutes longer at his post on Sunday evening, that ship might have had the proud distinction of rescuing the lives of the passengers and crew of the *Titanic*.

INTERNATIONAL SIGNALS OF DISTRESS AT SEA.

The committee deems it important to emphasize the meaning of signals of distress and includes in its report the international code, which is as follows:

SIGNALS OF DISTRESS.

When a vessel is in distress and requires assistance from other vessels or from the shore, the following shall be the signals to be used or displayed by her, either together or separately:

IN THE DAYTIME.

(1.) A gun or other explosive signal fired intervals of about a minute.

(2.) The international code signal of distress indicated by NC.

(3.) The distant signal, consisting of square flag, having either above or below it a ball or anything resembling a ball. (This is purely a code signal, and is not one of the signals of distress given in the

Rules of the Road, the needless exhibition of which entails penalties upon the master of the vessel displaying it.)

(4.) The distant signal, consisting of a cone, point upward, having either above it or below it a ball or anything resembling a ball.

(5.) A continuous sounding with any fog-signal apparatus.

AT NIGHT.

(1.) A gun or other explosive signal fired at intervals of about a minute.

(2.) Flames on the vessel (as from a burning tar barrel, oil barrel, etc.).

(3.) Rockets or shells, throwing stars of any color or description, fired one at a time at short intervals.

(4.) A continuous sounding with any fog-signal apparatus.

Abandoning Ship

STEAMSHIP *TITANIC'S* LIFEBOATS CLEARED AWAY.

When Captain Smith received the reports as to the water entering the ship, he promptly gave the order to clear away the lifeboats (p. 233), and later orders were given to put women and children into the boats. During this time distress rockets were fired at frequent intervals.

The lack of preparation was that this time most noticeable. There was no system adopted for loading the boats; there was great indecision as to the deck from which boats were to be loaded; there was wide diversity of opinion as to the number of the crew necessary to man each boat; there was no direction whatever as to the number of passengers to be carried by each boat, and no uniformity in loading them. On one side only women and children were put in the boats, while on the other side there was almost an equal proportion of men and women put into the boats, the women and children being given the preference in all cases. The failure to utilize all lifeboats to their recognized capacity for safety unquestionably resulted in the needless sacrifice of several hundred lives which might otherwise have been saved.

CAPACITY OF LIFEBOATS NOT UTILIZED.

The vessel was provided with lifeboats, as above stated, for 1,176 persons, while but 706 were saved. Only a few of the ship's lifeboats were fully loaded, while others were but partially filled. Some were loaded at the boat deck, and some at the A deck, and these were successfully lowered to the water. The twentieth boat was washed overboard when the forward part of the ship was submerged, and in its overturned condition served as a life raft for about 30 people, including Second Officer Lightoller, Wireless Operators Bride and Phillips (the latter dying before rescue), passengers Col. Gracie and Mr. Jack Thayer, and others of the crew, who climbed upon it from the water at about the time the ship disappeared.

LIFEBOAT DEVICES.

Had the sea been rough it is questionable whether any of the lifeboats of the *Titanic* would have reached the water without being damaged or destroyed. The point of suspension of the *Titanic*'s boats was about 70 feet above the level of the sea. Had the ship been rolling heavily the lifeboats as they were lowered would have swung out from the side of the ship as it rolled toward them and on the return roll would have swung back and crashed against its side. It is evident from the testimony that as the list of the *Titanic* became noticeable the lifeboats scraped against the high side as they were being lowered. Every effort should be made to improve boat handling devices, and to improve the control of boats while being lowered.

CONFLICT IN LIFEBOAT REPORTS.

In the reports of the survivors there are marked differences of opinion as to the number carried by each lifeboat. In No. 1, for instance, one survivor reports ten in all. The seaman in charge reports 7 crew and 14 to 20 passengers (p. 574). The officer who loaded this boat estimated that from 3 to 5 women and 22 men were aboard (pp. 404 and 405). Accepting the minimum report as made by any one survivor in every boat, the total far exceeds the actual number picked up by the *Carpathia*.

NO DISTINCTION BETWEEN PASSENGERS.

The testimony is definite that, except in isolated instances, there was no panic. In loading boats no distinction was made between first, second, and third class passengers, although the proportion of lost is larger among third class passengers than in either of the other classes. Women and children, without discrimination, were given preference.

Your committee believes that under proper discipline the survivors could have been concentrated into fewer boats after reaching the water, and we think that it would have been possible to have saved many lives had those in charge of the boats thus released returned promptly to the scene of the disaster.

CONDUCT ON LIFEBOATS.

After lowering, several of the boats rowed many hours in the direction of the lights supposed to have been displayed by the *Californian*. Other boats lay on their oars in the vicinity of the sinking ship, a few survivors being rescued from the water. After distributing his passengers among the four other boats which he had herded together, and after the cries of distress had died away, Fifth Officer Lowe, in boat No. 14, went to the scene of the wreck and rescued four living passengers from the water, one of whom afterwards died in the lifeboat, but was identified. Officer Lowe then set sail in boat No. 14, took in tow one collapsible boat, and proceeded to the rescue of passengers on another collapsible lifeboat.

The men who had taken refuge on the overturned collapsible lifeboat were rescued, including Second Officer Lightoller and passengers Gracie and Thayer, and Wireless Operators Bride and Phillips, by lifeboats No. 4 and No. 12, before the arrival of the *Carpathia*. The fourth collapsible lifeboat was rowed to the side of the *Carpathia*, and contained 28 women and children, mostly third class passengers, 3 firemen, 1 steward, 4 Filipinos, President Ismay, and Mr. Carter, of Philadelphia, and was in charge of Quartermaster Rowe.

SHIP SINKING.

The ship went down gradually by the bow, assuming an almost perpendicular position just before sinking at 12.47 a.m., New York time, April 15. There have been many conflicting statements as to whether the ship broke in two, but the preponderance of evidence is to the effect that she assumed an almost end-on position and sank intact. [We know today that the *Titanic* did in fact break into two sections as she sank, between the third and fourth funnels – Editor]

NO SUCTION.

The committee deems it of sufficient importance to call attention to the fact that as the ship disappeared under the water there was no apparent suction or unusual disturbance of the surface of the water. Testimony is abundant that while she was going down there was not sufficient suction to be manifest to any of the witnesses who were in the water or on the overturned collapsible boat or on the floating debris, or to the occupants of the lifeboats in the vicinity of the vessel, or to prevent those in the water, whether equipped with lifebelts or not, from easily swimming away from the ship's side while she was sinking.

The Rescue

CAPTAIN ROSTRON.

The committee invites your attention to the course followed by Captain Rostron, commanding the *Carpathia*. Immediately upon the receipt of the wireless call of distress Captain Rostron gave the order to turn the ship around and set a definite course toward the *Titanic* and instructed the Chief Engineer to call another watch of stokers and make all possible speed to that ship.

Realizing the possible presence of ice, because of the collision, Captain Rostron doubled his lookouts and exerted extra vigilance, putting an extra lookout on duty forward and having another officer on the bridge. The captain immediately instructed the first officer to "prepare all our lifeboats and have them all ready for turning outboard." He further sent for the heads of the different departments and issued the following order, which the committee deem of sufficient importance to quote in full:

English doctor, with assistants, to remain in first class dining room.

Italian doctor, with assistants, to remain in second class dining room.

Hungarian doctor, with assistants, to remain in third class dining room.

Each doctor to have supplies of restoratives, stimulants, and everything to hand for immediate needs of probable wounded or sick.

Purser, with assistant purser and chief steward, to receive the passengers, etc., at different gangways, controlling our own stewards in assisting *Titanic* passengers to the dining rooms, etc.; also to get Christian and surnames of all survivors as soon as possible to send by wireless.

Inspector, steerage stewards, and master at arms to control our own steerage passengers and keep them out of the third class dining hall, and also to keep them out of the way and off the deck to prevent confusion.

Chief steward: That all hands would be called and to have coffee, etc., ready to serve out to all our crew.

Have coffee, tea, soup, etc., in each saloon, blankets in saloons, at the gangways, and some for the boats.

To see all rescued cared for and immediate wants attended to.

My cabin and all officials' cabins to be given up. Smoke rooms, library, etc., dining rooms, would be utilized to accommodate the survivors.

All spare berths in steerage to be utilized for *Titanic*'s passengers, and get all our own steerage passengers grouped together.

Stewards to be placed in each alleyway to reassure our own passengers, should they inquire about noise in getting our boats out, etc., or the working of engines.

To all I strictly enjoined the necessity for order, discipline, and quietness, and to avoid all confusion.

Chief and first officers: All the hands to be called; get coffee, etc. Prepare and swing out all boats.

All gangway doors to be opened.

Electric sprays in each gangway and over side.

A block with line rove hooked in each gangway.

A chair sling at each gangway for getting up sick or wounded.

Boatswains' chairs, pilot ladders, and canvas ash bags to be at each gangway, the canvas ash bags for children.

Cargo falls with both ends clear; bowlines in the ends and bights secured along ship's sides for boat ropes or to help the people up.

Heaving lines distributed along the ship's side and gaskets handy near gangways for lashing people in chairs, etc.

Forward derricks topped and rigged and steam on winches; also told off officers for different stations and for certain eventualities.

Ordered company's rockets to be fired at 2.45 a.m. and every quarter of an hour after to reassure *Titanic*.

The committee deems the course followed by Captain Rostron of the *Carpathia* as deserving of the highest praise and worthy of especial recognition. Captain Rostron fully realized all the risk involved. He doubled his lookouts, doubled his fireroom force, and notwithstanding such risk, pushed his ship at her very highest limit of speed through the many dangers of the night to the relief of the stricken vessel. His detailed instructions issued in anticipation of the rescue of the *Titanic* are a marvel of systematic preparation and completeness, evincing such solicitude as calls for the highest commendation. The precautions he adopted enabled him to steer his course between and around icebergs until he stopped his engines at 4 o'clock in the morning in the vicinity of the accident, where he proceeded to pick up the *Titanic*'s lifeboats with the survivors.

ON THE SCENE OF THE RESCUE.

The first boat was picked up at 4.10 a.m. Monday, and the last of the survivors was on board by 8.30 a.m., after which Captain Rostron made arrangements "to hold service, a short prayer of thankfulness for those rescued, and a short burial service for those who were lost."

Upon the arrival of the *Californian* upon the scene, about 8 o'clock in the morning, the Captain of the *Carpathia* communicated with her commander, stating that all of the passengers had been rescued from the boats but that he thought one was still unaccounted for; and arrangements were made whereby the *Californian* made an exhaustive search in the vicinity for this missing boat.

Captain Rostron stated that the *Carpathia* picked up 15 lifeboats and 2 collapsible boats. Evidence was given before the committee by at least one occupant of every lifeboat, satisfying the committee that the 16 lifeboats with which the *Titanic* was equipped were all accounted for. Thirteen of these lifeboats were hoisted on board and carried to New York by the *Carpathia*.

After arranging for a thorough search of the vicinity by the *Californian*, Captain Rostron headed his vessel for New York, reporting immediately by wireless to the officials of his company in New York, as follows:

> NEW YORK, latitude 41.45; longitude 50.20 west. - Am proceeding New York unless otherwise ordered, with about 800, after having consulted with Mr. Ismay and considering the circumstances. With so much ice about, consider New York best. Large number icebergs, and 20 miles field ice with bergs amongst.

BODIES NOT VISIBLE.

The committee directs attention to the fact that Captain Rostron, of the *Carpathia*, although four hours in the vicinity of the accident, saw only one body, and that Captain Lord, of the *Californian*, who remained three hours in the vicinity of the wreckage, saw none. The failure of the captain of the *Carpathia*, of the captain of the *Californian*, and of the captain of the *Mount Temple* to find bodies floating in that vicinity in the early morning of the day following can only be accounted for on the theory that those who went down with the ship either did not rise to the surface or were carried away or hidden by the extensive ice floe which during the night came down over the spot where the ship disappeared, while those bodies which have been found remote from the place where the ship went down were probably carried away from the scene by the currents or by the movement of the ice.

Reporting Disaster

WIRELESS SERVICE.

Numerous wireless messages of an official character were given to the operator on the *Carpathia* on Monday morning, April 15, with explicit instructions from the captain to send them immediately, and, if necessary, relay through other vessels.

Captain Rostron's testimony on this point before the committee on April 19, 1912, the day following his arrival in New York, is unqualified upon this point, and is as follows:

> From the very commencement I took charge of the whole thing and issued orders that every message sent would be sent under my authority, and no message was to be sent unless authorized by me. My orders were: First of all, the two official messages. The two official messages were to the Cunard Co. and the White Star Co., as regards the accident, telling them that I had gotten approximate number of passengers aboard and was returning to New York. That was to the White Star Co., and the other one was to our company, of course, telling them that I was proceeding to New York unless otherwise ordered, and considered New York the best for many considerations.
>
> After those two messages were sent, I sent a press message to the Associated Press, practically in the same words as I had sent to the companies, over my signature.
>
> Those were the three first messages that were sent. After these messages were sent, we began sending in the names of the first class passengers. This was by the *Olympic* on Monday evening. We got the first, and, I think, all the second, off by the *Olympic*. Then we lost touch.
>
> I controlled the whole thing through my orders. I said I placed official messages first. After they had gone and the first press message, then the names of the passengers. After the names of the passengers and crew had been sent my orders were to send all private messages from the *Titanic*'s passengers first in the order in which they were given in to the purser; no preference to any message.

The question having arisen as to the authority exercised over the operator of the *Carpathia*, the chairman of the subcommittee sent the following cablegram to Captain Rostron:

NEW YORK, May 4, 1912.

To Captain ROSTRON,

Cunard Steamship "*Carpathia*," Gibraltar:

Original wireless message sent by Bruce Ismay addressed Islefrank, New York City, immediately after he boarded *Carpathia* Monday morning, April 15, containing these words, "Deeply regret advise you *Titanic* sank this morning after collision iceberg, resulting serious loss life. Further particulars later," signed Bruce Ismay, is now in my possession. Ismay under oath waived secrecy and I desire cable from you containing contents of that message and any memoranda thereon showing hour and date when sent by *Carpathia* operator and through what ship or shore station. Also whether relayed through other ship station. Also whether operator was forbidden by you to communicate such message or any other message via steamships *Californian* and *Olympic*. Also whether operator was prevented by you from sending this message or any other concerning accident. Cable answer collect to me, Washington.

WILLIAM ALDEN SMITH,

Chairman Senate Subcommittee.

And received the following reply:

GIBRALTAR, May 18, 1912.

Senator WILLIAM ALDEN SMITH,

Chairman Senate Subcommittee, Washington:

Ismay's telegram begins "Islefrank, New York; deeply regret advise you *Titanic* sunk this morning, 15th, alter collision with iceberg, resulting serious loss of life; further particulars later. Bruce Ismay, Exe." (ends). Purser asked my permission to send it, which I granted. As it was official message, Ismay mentally very ill at time, our purser asked him to add last three words; now find sent through Sable Island 17th April. Message given to purser afternoon of 15th; purser took message to Operator Cottam personally and gave my permission to send early as possible. I did not forbid relaying message to any ship. On contrary, particularly mentioned doing all possible to get official messages, names of survivors, then survivors' messages away by most convenient means. By *Olympic* were sent my messages signed by self to Cunard, Liverpool, and New York, White Star, and press messages, Ismay's, almost identical with mine; worked *Olympic* as long as possible. Only messages I prevented sending were further press messages. I desire full investigation my actions.

ROSTRON.

10.40 p.m.

Notwithstanding the specific instructions of the Captain to the Wireless Operator on the morning of April 15 regarding the transmission of Mr. Ismay's message to Mr. Franklin in New York, the evidence shows that the message in question was not received by Mr. Franklin until about 9 o'clock Wednesday morning, April 17. The original message, in the possession of the committee, shows that the message was transmitted from the *Carpathia*, April 17, via Halifax. Our investigation discloses the fact that the message was delivered to Mr. Franklin in New York promptly after its receipt by the Postal Telegraph & Cable Co.

The message in question is as follows:

STEAMSHIP *CARPATHIA*, April 17, 1912 (via Halifax).

ISLEFRANK, N. Y. C.:

Deeply regret advise you *Titanic* sank this morning, after collision iceberg, resulting serious loss life. Further particulars later.

BRUCE ISMAY.

This message was received by Mr. Franklin in New York about 9 a.m. April 17.

PUBLIC INFORMATION.

The record further discloses the first official information concerning the disaster communicated to the public by the officials of the White Star Line was received from Capt. Haddock, of the *Olympic*, at 6.16 p.m. Monday, April 15, as follows:

> *Carpathia* reached *Titanic's* position at daybreak. Found boats and wreckage only. *Titanic* had foundered about 2.20 a.m. in 41.46 north, 50.14 west. All her boats accounted for. About 675 souls saved, crew and passengers, latter nearly all women and children. Leyland Line steamship *Californian* remaining and searching position of disaster. *Carpathia* returning to New York with survivors; please inform Cunard.
>
> HADDOCK.

Notwithstanding this information in possession of the officials of that company, a telegram was sent to Representative J. A. Hughes, Huntington, W. Va., dated New York, April 15, 1912, rending as follows:

> Passengers will probably land there Wednesday all safe.
>
> WHITE STAR LINE.
>
> 8.27 p.m.

The committee have been unable to fix the identity of the author of this telegram. We find, however, that this message was delivered to the Western Union branch office, in the same building as the offices of the White Star Line, 11 Broadway, at 7.51 p.m., on that day, but are left wholly in doubt as to the person who sent it or the purpose of the author in sending such a message. Whoever sent this message, under the circumstances, is guilty of the most reprehensible conduct.

INFORMATION WITHHELD.

The committee does not believe that the wireless operator on the *Carpathia* showed proper vigilance in handling the important work confided to his care after the accident. Information concerning an accident at sea had been used by a Wireless Operator prior to this accident for his own advantage. That such procedure had been permitted by the Marconi Co. may have had its effect on this occasion. The disposition of officials of the Marconi Co. to permit this practice and the fact of that company's representatives making the arrangements for the sale of the experiences of the operators of the *Titanic* and *Carpathia* subjects the participants to criticism, and the practice should be prohibited. The committee are pleased to note that Mr. Marconi approves of such prohibition.

Recommendations

The committee finds that this accident clearly indicates the necessity of additional legislation to secure safety of life at sea.

By statute the United States accepts reciprocally the inspection certificates of foreign countries having inspection laws approximating those of the United States. Unless there is early revision of inspection laws of foreign countries along the lines laid down hereinafter, the committee deems it proper that such reciprocal arrangements be terminated, and that no vessel shall be licensed to carry passengers from ports of the United States until all regulations and requirements of the laws of the United States have been fully complied with.

The committee recommends that sections 4481 and 4488, Revised Statutes, be so amended as to definitely require sufficient lifeboats to accommodate every passenger and every member of the crew. That the importance of this feature is recognized by the steamship lines is indicated by the fact that on many lines steps are being taken to provide lifeboat capacity for every person on board, including crew; and the fact of such equipment is being widely advertised. The president of the International Mercantile Marine Co., Mr. Ismay, definitely stated to the committee (p. 985):

> We have issued instructions that none of the ships of our lines shall leave any port carrying more passengers and crew than they have capacity for in the lifeboats.
>
> Not less than four members of the crew, skilled in handling boats, should be assigned to every boat. All members of the crew assigned to lifeboats should be drilled in lowering and rowing the boats, not less than twice each month and the fact of such drill or practice should be noted in the log.

The committee recommends the assignment of passengers and crew to lifeboats before sailing; that occupants of certain groups of staterooms and the stewards of such groups of rooms be assigned to certain boats most conveniently located with reference to the rooms in question; the assignment of boats and the shortest route from stateroom to boat to be posted in every stateroom.

The committee recommends that every ocean steamship carrying 100 or more passengers be required to carry 2 electric searchlights.

The committee finds that this catastrophe makes glaringly apparent the necessity for regulation of radiotelegraphy. There must be an operator on duty at all times, day and night, to insure the immediate receipt of all distress, warning, or other important calls. Direct communication either by clear-speaking telephone, voice tube, or messenger must be provided between the wireless room and the bridge, so that the operator does not have to leave his station. There must be definite legislation to prevent interference by amateurs, and to secure secrecy of radiograms or wireless messages. There must be some source of auxiliary power, either storage battery or oil engine, to insure the operation of the wireless installation until the wireless room is submerged.

The committee recommends the early passage of S. 6412, already passed by the Senate and favorably reported by the House.

The committee recommends that the firing of rockets or candles on the high seas for any other purpose than as a signal of distress be made a misdemeanor.

The committee recommends that the following additional structural requirements be required as regards ocean-going passenger steamers the construction of which is begun after this date:

All steel ocean and coastwise seagoing ships carrying 100 or more passengers should have a watertight skin inboard of the outside plating, extending not less than 10 percent of the load draft above the full-load waterline, either in the form of an inner bottom or of longitudinal watertight bulkheads, and this construction should extend from the forward collision bulkhead over not less than two-thirds of the length of the ship.

All steel ocean and coastwise seagoing ships carrying 100 or more passengers should have bulkheads so spaced that any two adjacent compartments of the ship may be flooded without destroying the flotability or stability of the ship. Watertight transverse bulkheads should extend from side to side of the ship, attaching to the outside shell. The transverse bulkheads forward and abaft the machinery spaces should he continued watertight vertically to the uppermost continuous structural deck. The uppermost continuous structural deck should be fitted watertight. Bulkheads within the limits of the machinery spaces should extend not less than 25 percent of the draft of the ship above the load waterline and should end at a watertight deck. All watertight bulkheads and decks should be proportioned to withstand, without material permanent deflection, a water pressure equal to 5 feet more than the full height of the bulkhead. Bulkheads of novel dimensions or scantlings should be tested by being subjected to actual water pressure.

British Wreck Commissioner's Inquiry
Report on the Loss of the *Titanic*. (s.s.)

THE MERCHANT SHIPPING ACTS, 1894 TO 1906.

IN THE MATTER OF the Formal Investigation held at the Scottish Hall, Buckingham Gate, Westminster, on the 2nd, 3rd, 7th, 8th, 9th, 10th, 14th, 15th, 16th, 17th, 20th, 21st, 22nd, 23rd, and 24th May, the 4th, 5th, 6th, 7th, 10th, 11th, 12th, 13th, 14th, 17th, 18th, 19th, 21st, 24th, 25th, 26th, 27th, 28th, and 29th June, at the Caxton Hall, Caxton Street, Westminster, on the 1st and 3rd July, and at the Scottish Hall, Buckingham Gate, Westminster, on the 30th July, 1912, before the Right Honourable Lord Mersey, Wreck Commissioner, assisted by Rear Admiral the Honourable S. A. Gough-Calthorpe, C.V.O., R.N.; Captain A. W. Clarke; Commander F. C. A. Lyon, R.N.R.; Professor J. H. Biles, D.Sc., LL.D.; and Mr. E. C. Chaston, R.N.R., as Assessors, into the circumstances attending the loss of the steamship *Titanic* of Liverpool, and the loss of 1,490 lives in the North Atlantic Ocean, in lat. 41 deg; 46' N., long. 50 deg; 14' W. on the 15th April last.

REPORT OF THE COURT.

The Court, having carefully inquired into the circumstances of the above mentioned shipping casualty, finds, for the reasons appearing in the annex hereto, that the loss of the said ship was due to collision with an iceberg, brought about by the excessive speed at which the ship was being navigated.

Dated this 30th day of July, 1912.

MERSEY.

Wreck Commissioner.

We concur in the above report.

ARTHUR GOUGH-CALTHORPE,

A. W. CLARKE,

F. C. A. LYON,

J. H. BILES,

EDWARD C. CHASTON.

Assessors.

Description of the Ship
The White Star Line

The *Titanic* was one of a fleet of thirteen ships employed in the transport of passengers, mails, and cargo between Great Britain and the United States, the usual ports of call for the service in which she was engaged being Southampton, Cherbourg, Plymouth, Queenstown, and New York. (Sanderson, 19589-97)

The owners are the Oceanic Steam Navigation Company, Limited, usually known as the White Star Line, a British registered company, with a capital of £750,000, all paid up, the directors being Mr. J. Bruce Ismay (Chairman), the Right Hon. Lord Pirrie, and Mr. H. A. Sanderson. (Ismay, 18224-69)

The Company are owners of twenty-nine steamers and tenders; they have a large interest in thirteen other steamers, and also own a training sailing ship for officers.

All of the shares of the Company, with the exception of eight held by Messrs. E. C. Grenfell, Vivian H. Smith, W. S. M. Burns, James Gray, J. Bruce Ismay, H. A. Sanderson, A. Kerr, and the Right Hon. Lord Pirrie, have, since the year 1902, been held by the International Navigation Company, Limited, of Liverpool, a British registered company, with a capital of £700,000, of which all is paid up, the directors being Mr. J. Bruce Ismay (Chairman), and Messrs. H. A. Sanderson, Charles F. Torrey, and H. Concanon.

The debentures of the Company, £1,250,000, are held mainly, if not entirely, in the United Kingdom by the general public.

The International Navigation Company, Limited, of Liverpool, in addition to holding the above-mentioned shares of the Oceanic Steam Navigation Company, Limited, is also the owner of:

1. Practically the whole of the issued share capital of the British and North Atlantic Steam Navigation Company, Limited, and the Mississippi and Dominion Steamship Company, Limited (the Dominion Line).

2. Practically the whole of the issued share capital of the Atlantic Transport Company, Limited (the Atlantic Transport Line).

3. Practically the whole of the issued ordinary share capital and about one-half of the preference share capital of Frederick Leyland and Company, Limited (the Leyland Line).

As against the above-mentioned shares and other property, the International Navigation Company, Limited, have issued share lien certificates for £25,000,000.

Both the shares and share lien certificates of the International Navigation Company, Limited, are now held by the International Mercantile Marine Company of New Jersey, or by trustees for the holders of its debenture bonds.

Description of the Ship

The *Titanic* was a three-screw vessel of 46,328 tons gross and 21,831 net register tons, built by Messrs. Harland and Wolff for the

White Star Line service between Southampton and New York She was registered as a British steamship at the port of Liverpool , her official number being 131,428. Her registered dimensions were: (Wilding, 19789)

Length.. 852·5 ft.
Breadth..92·5 "
Depth from top of keel to top of beam at lowest point of sheer of C. deck, the highest deck which extends continuously from bow to stern....................64ft. 9in.
Depth of hold,.. 59·58 ft.
Height from B to C deck...9·0
Height from A to B deck...9·0
Height from Boat to A deck...9·5
Height from Boat deck to waterline amidships at time of accident about................60·5"
Displacement at 34 ft. 7 in. is... 52,310 tons.

The propelling machinery consisted of two sets of four-cylinder reciprocating engines, each driving a wing propeller, and a turbine driving the centre propeller. The registered horsepower of the propelling machinery was 50,000. The power which would probably have been developed was at least 55,000.

Structural arrangements - The structural arrangements of the *Titanic* consisted primarily of:

(1) An outer shell of steel plating, giving form to the ship up to the top decks.

(2) Steel Decks. - These were enumerated as follows:

	Height to next deck above.	Distance from 34 ft. 7 in. waterline amidships.	
	Ft. In.	Above. Ft. In.	Below. Ft. In.
Boat deck, length about 500 ft.	- -	58 0	- -
A deck, length about 500 ft.	9 6	48 6	- -
B deck, length about 550 ft. with 125 ft.	9 0	39 6	- -

Deck			
forecastle and 105 ft. poop			
C deck, whole length of ship.	9 0	30 6	- -
D deck, whole length of ship.	10 6	20 0 (tapered down at ends)	- -
E deck, whole length of ship.	9 0	11 0	5 6
F deck, whole length of ship.	8 6	2 6	13 6
G deck, 190 ft. forward of boilers, 210 ft. aft of machinery	8 0	- -	- -
Orlop deck, 190 ft. forward of boilers, 210 ft. aft of machinery	8 0	- -	- -

C D, E and F were continuous from end to end of the ship. The decks above these were continuous for the greater part of the ship, extending from amidships both forward and aft. The Boat deck and A deck each had two expansion joints, which broke the strength continuity. The decks below were continuous outside the boiler and engine rooms and extended to the ends of the ship. Except in small patches none of these decks was watertight in the steel parts, except the weather deck and the Orlop deck aft.

(3) Transverse Vertical Bulkheads. - There were 15 transverse watertight bulkheads, by which the ship was divided in the direction of her length into 16 separate compartments. These bulkheads are referred to as "A" to "P," commencing forward.

The watertightness of the bulkheads extended up to one or other of the decks D or E; the bulkhead A extended to C, but was only watertight to D deck. The position of the D, E and F decks, which were the only ones to which the watertight bulkheads extended was in relation to the waterline (34 ft. 7 in. draught) approximately as follows:

Height above waterline (34 ft. 7 in.).

	Lowest part amidships.		At bow.		At stern.	
	Feet	Inches	Feet	Inches	Feet	Inches
D	20	0	33	0 25	0	
E	11	0	24	0 16	0	
F	2	6	25	6 7	6	

These were the three of the four decks which, as already stated, were continuous all fore and aft. The other decks, G and Orlop, which extended only along a part of the ship, were spaced about 8 ft. apart. The G deck forward was about 7 ft. 6 in. above the waterline at the bow and about level with the waterline at bulkhead D, which was at the fore end of boilers. The G deck aft and the Orlop deck at both ends of the vessel were below the waterline. The Orlop deck abaft of the turbine engine-room and forward of the collision bulkhead was watertight. Elsewhere, except in very small patches, the decks were not watertight. All the decks had large openings or hatchways in them in each compartment, so that water could rise freely through them.

There was also a watertight inner bottom, or tank top, about 5 ft. above the top of the keel, which extended for the full breadth of the vessel from bulkhead A to 20 ft. before bulkhead P - i.e., for the whole length of the vessel except a small distance at each end. The transverse watertight divisions of this double bottom practically coincided with the watertight transverse bulkheads; there was an additional watertight division under the middle of the reciprocating engine room compartment (between bulkheads K and L). There were three longitudinal watertight divisions in the double bottom, one at the centre of the ship, extending for about 670 ft., and one on each side, extending for 447 ft.

All the transverse bulkheads were carried up watertight to at least the height of the E deck. Bulkheads A and B, and all bulkheads from K (90 ft. abaft amidships) to P, both inclusive, further extended watertight up to the underside of D deck. A bulkhead further extended to C deck, but it was watertight only to D deck.

Bulkheads A and B forward, and P aft, had no openings in them. All the other bulkheads had openings in them, which were fitted with watertight doors. Bulkheads D to O, both inclusive, had each a vertical sliding watertight door at the level of the floor of the engine and boiler rooms for the use of the engineers and firemen. On the Orlop deck there was one door, on bulkhead N, for access to the refrigerator rooms. On G deck there were no watertight doors in the bulkheads. On both the F and E decks nearly all the bulkheads had watertight doors, mainly for giving communication between the different blocks of passenger accommodation.

All the doors, except those in the engine rooms and boiler rooms, were horizontal sliding doors workable by hand both at the door and at the deck above.

There were twelve vertical sliding watertight doors which completed the watertightness of bulkheads D to O inclusive, in the boiler and engine rooms. These were capable of being simultaneously closed from the bridge. The operation of closing was intended to be preceded by the ringing from the bridge of a warning bell.

These doors were closed by the bringing into operation of an electric current and could not be opened until this current was cut off from the bridge. When this was done the doors could only be opened by a mechanical operation manually worked separately at each door. They could, however, be individually lowered again by operating a lever at the door. In addition they would be automatically closed, if open, should water enter the compartment. This operation was done in each case by means of a float actuated by the water which was in either of the compartments which happened to be in the process of being flooded.

There were no sluice valves or means of letting water from one compartment to another.

Watertight Compartments.

The following is a more detailed description of the vessel, her passenger and crew accommodation, and her machinery.

Watertight compartments.

The following table shows the decks to which the bulkheads extended, and the numbers of doors in them:

Bulkhead letter.	Extends up to under side of Deck.	Engine and boiler spaces (all controlled from bridge).	Orlop to G deck.	F to E deck.	E to D deck.
A	C	-	-	-	-
B	D	-	-	-	-
C	E	-	-	1	-
D	E	* 1	-	1	-
E	E	†1	-	1	-
F	E	†1	-	2	-
G	E	†1	-	1	-
H	E	†1	-	2	-
J	E	†1	-	2	-
K	D	1	-	-	2
L	D	1	-	-	2
M	D	1	-	1	2
N	D	1	1	1	2
O	D	1	-	-	1
P	D		-		-

* There was another watertight door at the after end of the watertight passage through the bunker immediately aft of "D" bulkhead. This door and the one on the "D" bulkhead formed a double protection to the forward boiler room.

† The watertight doors for these bulkheads were not on them, but were at the end of a watertight passage (about 9 feet long), leading from the bulkhead through the bunker into the compartment.

The following table shows the actual contents of each separate watertight compartment. The compartments are shown in the left column, the contents of each compartment being read off horizontally. The contents of each watertight compartment is separately given in the deck space in which it is:

W. T. compt.	Length of each W T compt. In fore and aft direction.	Hold.	Orlop to G deck.	G to F deck.	F to E deck.	E to D deck.
Bow to A	46 ft.	Forepeak tank - not used except for trimming ship	Forepeak storeroom	Forepeak storeroom	Forepeak storeroom	Forepeak storeroom
A - B	45 ft.	Cargo	Cargo	Living spaces for firemen, etc.	Living spaces for firemen	Living spaces for firemen
B - C	51 ft.	Do.	Do.	3rd class passenger accommodation	3rd class passenger accommodation	3rd class passenger accommodation
C - D	51 ft.	Alternatively coal and cargo	Luggage and mails	Baggage, squash rackets and 3rd class passengers	3rd class passenger accommodation	3rd class passenger accommodation
D - E	54 ft.	No. 6 boiler-room	No. 6 boiler-room	Coal and boiler casing	3rd class passenger accommodation	3rd class passenger accommodation

The Titanic Reports

E - F	57 ft.	No. 5 do.	No. 5 do.	Coal bunker and boiler casing and swimming bath	Linen rooms and swimming bath		3rd class passenger accommodation
F - G	57 ft.	No. 4 do.	No. 4 do.	Coal bunker and boiler casing	Stewards, Turkish baths, etc.		1st class passenger accommodation
G - H	57 ft.	No. 3 do.	No. 3 do.	Coal bunker and boiler casing	3rd class saloon		1st class passenger accommodation
H - J	60 ft.	No. 2 do.	No. 2 do.	Coal bunker and boiler casing	3rd class saloon		1st class and stewards
J - K	36 ft.	No. 1 do.	No. 1 do.	Coal bunker and boiler casing	3rd class galley, stewards, etc.		1st and 2nd class and stewards
K - L	69 ft.	Recipg. Engine room	Recipg. Engine room	Recipg. Engine room casing, work shop and engineers' stores	Engineers' and Recipg. Engine casing		1st class
L - M	57 ft.	Turbine engine room	Turbine engine room	Turbine engine room casing and small stewards str	2nd class and turbine eng. Room casing		1st class and stewards

M - N	63 ft.	Electric engine room	Provisions and electric engine casing	Provisions	2nd class	1st class and engineers' mess, &c.
N - O	54 ft.	Tunnel	Refrigerated cargo	3rd class	2nd class	2nd class and stewards, &c.
O - P	57 ft.	Do.	Cargo	3rd class	3rd class	2nd and 3rd class
P to stern.	36 ft.	After peak tank for trimming ship	After peak tank for trimming ship	Stores	Stores	Stores

The vessel was constructed under survey of the British Board of Trade for a passenger certificate, and also to comply with the American Immigration Laws

Steam was supplied from six entirely independent groups of boilers in six separate watertight compartments. The after boiler room, No. 1, contained five single-ended boilers. Four other boiler rooms, Nos. 2, 3, 4 and 5, each contained five double-ended boilers. The forward boiler room, No. 6, contained four double-ended boilers. The reciprocating engines and most of the auxiliary machinery were in a seventh separate watertight compartment aft of the boilers; the low-pressure turbine, the main condensers and the thrust blocks of the reciprocating engine were in an eighth separate watertight compartment. The main electrical machinery was in a ninth separate watertight compartment immediately abaft the turbine engine room. Two emergency steam-driven dynamos were placed on the D deck, 21 ft. above the level of the load waterline. These dynamos were arranged to take their supply of steam from any of the three of the boiler rooms Nos. 2, 3 and 5, and were intended to be available in the event of the main dynamo room being flooded.

The ship was equipped with the following:

(1) Wireless telegraphy.

(2) Submarine signalling.

(3) Electric lights and power systems.

(4) Telephones for communication between the different working positions in the vessel. In addition to the telephones, the means of communication included engine and docking telegraphs, and duplicate or emergency engine room telegraph, to be used in the event of any accident to the ordinary telegraph.

(5) Three electric elevators for taking passengers in the first class up to A deck, immediately below the Boat deck, and one in the second class for taking passengers up to the Boat deck.

(6) Four electrically-driven boat winches on the Boat deck for hauling up the boats.

(7) Life-saving appliances to the requirements of the Board of Trade, including boats and lifebelts.

(8) Steam whistles on the two foremost funnels, worked on the Willett-Bruce system of automatic control.

(9) Navigation appliances, including Kelvin's patent sounding machines for finding the depth of water under the ship without stopping; Walker's taffrail log for determining the speed of the ship; and flash signal lamps fitted above the shelters at each end of the navigating bridge for Morse signalling with other ships.

Decks and Accommodation

The Boat Deck was an uncovered deck, on which the boats were placed. At its lowest point it was about 92 ft. 6 in. above the keel. The overall length of this deck was about 500 ft. The forward end of it was fitted to serve as the navigating bridge of the vessel and was 190 ft. from the bow. On the after end of the bridge was a wheel house, containing the steering wheel and a steering compass. The chart room was immediately abaft this. On the starboard side of the wheel house and funnel casing were the navigating room, the captain's quarters, and some officers' quarters. On the port side were the remainder of the officers' quarters. At the middle line abaft the forward funnel casing were the wireless telegraphy rooms and the operators' quarters. The top of the officers' house formed a short deck. The connections from the Marconi aerials were made on this deck, and two of the collapsible boats were placed on it. Aft of the officers' house were the first class passengers' entrance and stairways, and other adjuncts to the passengers' accommodation below. These stairways had a minimum effective width of 8 ft. They had assembling landings at the level of each deck, and three elevators communicating from E to A decks, but not to the Boat deck, immediately on the fore side of the stairway.

All the boats except two Englehardt life rafts were carried on this deck. There were seven lifeboats on each side, 30 ft. long, 9 ft. wide. There was an emergency cutter, 25 ft. long, on each side at the fore end of the deck. Abreast of each cutter was an Englehardt life raft. One similar raft was carried on the top of the officers' house on each side. In all there were 14 lifeboats, 2 cutters, and 4 Englehardt life rafts.

The forward group of four boats and one Englehardt raft were placed on each side of the deck alongside the officers' quarters and the first class entrance. Further aft at the middle line on this deck was the special platform for the standard compass. At the after end of this deck was an entrance house for second class passengers, with a stairway and elevator leading directly down to F deck. There were two vertical iron ladders at the after-end of this deck, leading to A deck, for the use of the crew. Alongside and immediately forward of the second class entrance was the after group of lifeboats, four on each side of the ship.

In addition to the main stairways mentioned, there was a ladder on each side amidships, giving access from the A deck below. At the forward end of the Boat deck there was on each side a ladder leading up from A deck, with a landing there, from which, by a ladder, access to B deck could be obtained direct. Between the reciprocating engine casing and the third funnel casing there was a stewards' stairway, which communicated with all the decks below as far as E deck. Outside the deck houses was promenading space for first class passengers.

A Deck. - The next deck below the Boat deck was A deck. It extended over a length of about 500 feet. On this deck was a long house, extending nearly the whole length of the deck. It was of irregular shape, varying in width from 24 ft. to 72 ft. At the forward end it contained 34 state-rooms, and abaft these a number of public rooms, etc., for first class passengers, including two first class entrances and stairway, reading room, lounge and the smoke room. Outside the deck house was a promenade for first class passengers. The forward end of it on both sides of the ship, below the forward group of boats and for a short distance further aft, was protected against the weather by a steel screen, 192 ft. long, with large windows in it. In addition to the stairway described on the Boat deck, there was near the after-end of the A deck, and immediately forward of the first class smoke room, another first class entrance, giving access as far down as C deck. The second class stairway the after-end of this deck (already described under the Boat deck) had no exit on to the A deck. The stewards' staircase opened on to this deck.

B Deck. - The next lowest deck was B deck, which constituted the top deck of the strong structure of the vessel, the decks above and the side plating between them being light plating. This deck extended continuously for 550 ft. There were breaks or wells both forward and aft of it, each about 50 ft. long. It was terminated by a poop and forecastle. On this deck were placed the principal staterooms of the vessel, 97 in number, having berths for 198 passengers, and aft of these was the first class stairway and reception room, as well as the restaurant for first class passengers and its pantry and galley. Immediately aft of this restaurant were the second class stairway and smoke room. At the forward end of the deck outside the house was an assembling area, giving access by the ladders, previously mentioned, leading directly to the Boat deck. From this same space a ladderway led to the forward third class promenade on C deck. At the after-end of it were two ladders giving access to the after third class promenade on C deck. At the after-end of this deck, at the middle line, was placed another second class stairway, which gave access to C, D, E, F and G decks.

At the forward end of the vessel, on the level of the B deck, was situated the forecastle deck, which was 125 ft. long. On it were placed the gear for working the anchors and cables and for warping (or moving) the ship in dock. At the after-end, on the same level, was the poop deck, about 105 ft. long, which carried the after-warping appliances and was a third class promenading space. Arranged above the poop was a light docking bridge, with telephone, telegraphs, etc., communicating to the main navigating bridge forward.

C Deck. - The next lowest deck was C deck. This was the highest deck which extended continuously from bow to stern. At the forward end of it, under the forecastle, was placed the machinery required for working the anchors and cables and for the warping of the ship referred to on B deck above: there were also the crew's galley and the seamen's and firemen's mess room accommodation, where their meals were taken. At the after-end of the forecastle, at each side of the ship, were the entrances to the third class spaces below. On the port side, at the extreme after-end and opening on to the deck, was the lamp room. The break in B deck between the forecastle and the first class passenger quarters formed a well about 50 ft. in length, which enabled the space under it on C deck to be used as a third class promenade. This space contained two hatchways, the No. 2 hatch and the bunker hatch. The latter of these hatchways gave access to the space allotted to the first and second class baggage hold, the mails, specie and parcel room, and to the lower hold, which was used for cargo or coals. Abaft of this well there was a house 450 ft. long and extending for the full breadth of the ship. It contained 148 staterooms for first class, besides service rooms of various kinds. On this deck, at the forward first class entrance, were the purser's office and the enquiry office, where passengers' telegrams were received for sending by the Marconi apparatus. Exit doors through the ship's side were fitted abreast of this entrance. Abaft the after-end of this long house was a promenade at the ship's side for second class passengers, sheltered by bulwarks and bulkheads. In the middle of the promenade stood the second class library. The two second class stairways were at the ends of the library, so that from the promenade access was obtained at each end to a second class main stairway. There was also access by a door from this space into each of the alleyways in the first class accommodation on each side of the ship, and by two doors at the after-end into the after-well. This after-well was about 50 ft. in length and contained two hatchways called No. 5 and No. 6 hatches. Abaft this well, under the poop, was the main third class entrance for the after-end of the vessel, leading directly down to G deck, with landings and access at each deck. The effective width of this stairway was 16 ft. to E deck. From E to F it was 8 ft. wide. Aft of this entrance on B deck were the third class smoke room and the general room. Between these rooms and the stern was the steam steering gear and the machinery for working the after capstan gear, which was used for warping the after-end of the vessel. The steam steering gear had three cylinders. The engines were in duplicate, to provide for the possibility of breakdown of one set.

D Deck. - The general height from D deck to C deck was 10 ft. 6 in., this being reduced to 9 ft. at the forward end, and 9 ft. 6 in. at the after end, the taper being obtained gradually by increasing the sheer of the D deck. The forward end of this deck provided accommodation for 108 firemen, who were in two separate watches. There was the necessary lavatory accommodation, abaft the firemen's quarters at the sides of the ship. On each side of the middle line immediately abaft the firemen's quarters there was a vertical spiral staircase leading to the forward end of a tunnel, immediately above the tank top, which extended from the foot of the staircase to the forward stokehole, so that the firemen could pass direct to their work without going through any passenger accommodation or over any passenger decks. On D deck abaft of this staircase was the third class promenade space which was covered in by C deck. From this promenade space there were four separate ladderways with two ladders, 4 ft. wide to each. One ladderway on each side forward led to C deck, and one, the starboard, led to E deck and continued to F deck as a double ladder and to G deck as a single ladder. The two ladder ways at the after end led to E deck on both sides and to F deck on the port side. Abaft this promenade space came a block of 50 first class staterooms. This surrounded the forward funnel. The main first class reception room and dining saloon were aft of these rooms and surrounded the No. 2 funnel. The reception room and staircase occupied 83 ft. of the length of the ship. The dining saloon occupied 112 ft., and was between the second and third funnels. Abaft this came the first class pantry, which occupied 56 ft. of the length of the ship. The reciprocating engine hatch came up through this pantry.

Aft of the first class pantry, the galley, which provides for both first and second class passengers, occupied 45 ft. of the length of the ship. Aft of this were the turbine engine hatch and the emergency dynamos. Abaft of and on the port side of this hatch were the second class pantry and other spaces used for the saloon service of the passengers. On the starboard side abreast of these there was a series of rooms used for hospitals and their attendants. These spaces occupied about 54 ft. of the length. Aft of these was the second class saloon occupying 70 ft. of the length. In the next 88 ft. of length there were 38 second class rooms and the necessary baths and lavatories. From here to the stern was accommodation for third class passengers and the main third class lavatories for the passengers in the after end of the ship. The watertight bulkheads come up to this deck throughout the length from the stern as far forward as the bulkhead dividing the after boiler room from the reciprocating engine room. The watertight bulkhead of the two compartments abaft the stern was carried up to this deck.

E Deck. - The watertight bulkheads, other than those mentioned as extending to D deck, all stopped at this deck. At the forward end was provided accommodation for three watches of trimmers, in three separate compartments, each holding 24 trimmers. Abaft this, on the port side, was accommodation for 44 seamen. Aft of this, and also on the starboard side of it, were the lavatories for crew and third class passengers; further aft again came the forward third class lavatories. Immediately aft of this was a passageway right across the ship communicating directly with the ladderways leading to the decks above and below and gangway doors in the ship's side. This passage was 9 ft. wide at the sides and 15 ft. at the centre of the ship.

From the after end of this cross passage main alleyways on each side of the ship ran right through to the after end of the vessel. That on the port side was about 8 1/2 ft. wide. It was the general communication passage for the crew and third class passengers and was known as the "working passage." In this passage at the centre line in the middle of the length of the ship direct access was obtained to the third class dining rooms on the deck below by means of a ladderway 20 ft. wide. Between the working passage and the ship's side was the accommodation for the petty officers, most of the stewards, and the engineers' mess room. This accommodation extended for 475 ft. From this passage access was obtained to both engine rooms and the engineers' accommodation, some third class lavatories and also some third class accommodation at the after end. There was another cross passage at the end of this accommodation about 9 ft. wide, terminating in gangway doors on each side of the ship. The port side of it was for third class passengers and the starboard for second class. A door divided the parts, but it could be opened for any useful purpose, or for an emergency. The second class stairway leading to the Boat deck was in the cross passage way.

The passage on the starboard side ran through the first and then the second class accommodation, and the forward main first class stairway and elevators extended to this deck, whilst both the second class main stairways were also in communication with this starboard passage. There were four first class, eight first or second alternatively, and 19 second class rooms leading off this starboard passage.

The remainder of the deck was appropriated to third class accommodation. This contained the bulk of the third class accommodation. At the forward end of it was the accommodation for 53 firemen constituting the third watch. Aft of this in three watertight compartments there was third class accommodation extending to 147 ft. In the next watertight compartment were the swimming bath and linen rooms. In the next watertight compartments were stewards' accommodation on the port side, and the Turkish baths on the starboard side. The next two watertight compartments each contained a third class dining room.

The third class stewards' accommodation, together with the third class galley and pantries, filled the watertight compartment. The engineers' accommodation was in the next compartment directly alongside the casing of the reciprocating engine room. The next three compartments were allotted to 64 second class staterooms. These communicated direct with the second class main stairways. The after compartments contained third class accommodation. All spaces on this deck had direct ladderway communication with the deck above, so that if it became necessary to close the watertight doors in the bulkheads an escape was available in all cases. On this deck in way of the boiler rooms were placed the electrically-driven fans which provided ventilation to the stokeholds.

G Deck. - The forward end of this deck had accommodation for 15 leading firemen and 30 greasers. The next watertight compartment contained third class accommodation in 26 rooms for 106 people. The next watertight compartment contained the first class baggage room, the post office accommodation, a racquet court, and seven third class rooms for 34 passengers. From this point to the after end of the boiler room the space was used for the 'tween deck bunkers. Alongside the reciprocating engine room were the engineers' stores and workshop. Abreast of the turbine engine room were some of the ship's stores. In the next watertight compartment abaft the turbine room were the main body of the stores. The next two compartments were appropriated to 186 third class passengers in 60 rooms; this deck was the lowest on which any passengers or crew were carried.

Below G Deck. - were two partial decks, the Orlop and Lower Orlop decks, the latter extending only through the forepeak and No. 1 hold; on the former deck, abaft the turbine engine room, were some store rooms containing stores for ship's use.

Below these decks again came the inner bottom, extending fore and aft through about nine-tenths of the vessel's length, and on this were placed the boilers, main and auxiliary machinery and the electric light machines. In the remaining spaces below G deck were cargo holds or 'tween decks, seven in all, six forward and one aft. The firemen's passage, giving direct access from their accommodation to the forward boiler room by stairs at the forward end, contained the various pipes and valves connected with the pumping arrangements at the forward end of the ship, and also the steam pipes conveying steam to the windlass gear forward and exhaust steam pipes leading from winches and other deck machinery. It was made thoroughly watertight throughout its length, and at its after-end was closed by a watertight vertical sliding door of the same character as other doors on the inner bottom. Special arrangements were made for pumping this space out, if necessary. The pipes were placed in this tunnel to protect them from possible damage by coal or cargo, and also to facilitate access to them.

On the decks was provided generally, in the manner above described, accommodation for a maximum number of 1,034 first class passengers, and at the same time 510 second class passengers and 1,022 third class passengers. Some of the accommodation was of an alternative character, and could be used for either of two classes of passengers. In the statement of figures the higher alternative class has been reckoned. This makes a total accommodation for 2,566 passengers.

Accommodation was provided for the crew as follows; about 75 of the deck department, including officers and doctors, 326 of the engine room department, including engineers, and 544 of the victualling department, including pursers and leading stewards.

Access of passengers to the Boat deck. - The following routes led directly from the various parts of the first class passenger accommodation to the Boat deck: From the forward ends of A, B, C,

D, and E decks by the staircase in the forward first class entrance direct to the Boat deck. The elevators led from the same decks as far as A deck, where further access was obtained by going up the top flight of the main staircase.

The same route was available for first class passengers forward of midships on B, C, and E decks.

First class passengers abaft amidships on B and C decks could use the staircase in the after main entrance to A deck, and then could pass out on to the deck, and by the midships stairs besides the house ascend to the Boat deck. They could also use the stewards' staircase between the reciprocating engine casing and Nos. 1 and 2 boiler casing, which led direct to the Boat deck. This last route was also available for passengers on E deck in the same divisions who could use the forward first class main stairway and elevators.

Second class passengers on D deck could use their own after-stairway to B deck, and could then pass up their forward stairway to the Boat deck, or else could cross their saloon and use the same stairway throughout.

Of the second class passengers on E deck, those abreast of the reciprocating engine casing, unless the watertight door immediately abaft them was closed, went aft and joined the other second class passengers. If, however, the watertight door at the end of their compartment was closed, they passed through an emergency door into the engine room, and directly up to the Boat deck, by the ladders and gratings in the engine room casing.

The second class passengers on E deck in the compartment abreast the turbine casing on the starboard side, and also those on F deck on both sides below could pass through M watertight bulkhead to the forward second class main stairway. If this door were closed, they could pass by the stairway up to the serving space at the forward end of the second class saloon, and go into the saloon and thence up the forward second class stairway.

Passengers between M and N bulkheads on both E and F decks could pass directly up to the forward second class stairway to the Boat deck.

Passengers between N and O bulkheads on D, E, F and G decks could pass by the after second class stairway to B deck, and then cross to the forward second class stairway and go up to the Boat deck.

Third class passengers at the fore end of the vessel could pass by the staircases to C deck in the forward well and by ladders on the port and starboard sides at the forward end of the deck houses, thence direct to the Boat deck outside the officers' accommodation. They might also pass along the working passage on E deck and through the emergency door to the forward first class main stairway, or through the door on the same deck at the forward end of the first class alleyway and up the first class stairway direct to the Boat deck.

The third class passengers at the after-end of the ship passed up their stairway to E deck, and into the working passage, and through the emergency doors to the two second class stairways, and so to the Boat deck, like second class passengers. Or, alternatively, they could continue up their own stairs and entrance to C deck, thence by the two ladders at the after-end of the bridge on to the B deck, and thence by the forward second class stairway direct to the Boat deck.

Crew. - From each boiler room an escape or emergency ladder was provided direct to the Boat deck by the fidleys, in the boiler casings, and also into the working passage on E deck, and thence by the stair immediately forward of the reciprocating engine casing, direct to the Boat deck.

From both the engine rooms ladders and gratings gave direct access to the Boat deck.

From the electric engine room, the after tunnels, and the forward pipe tunnels, escapes were provided direct to the working passage on E deck, and thence by one of the several routes already detailed from that space.

From the crew's quarters they could go forward by their own staircases into the forward well, and thence, like the third class passengers, to the Boat deck.

The stewards' accommodation being all connected to the working passage or the forward main first class stairway, they could use one of the routes from thence.

The engineers' accommodation also communicated with the working passage, but, as it was possible for them to be shut between two watertight bulkheads, they had also a direct route by the gratings in the engine room casing to the Boat deck.

On all the principal accommodation decks the alleyways and stairways provided a ready means of access to the Boat deck, and there were clear deck spaces in way of all first, second and third class main entrances and stairways on Boat deck and all decks below.

Structure

The vessel was built throughout of steel and had a cellular double bottom of the usual type, with a floor at every frame, its depth at the centre line being 63 in., except in way of the reciprocating machinery, where it was 78 in. For about half of the length of the vessel this double bottom extended up the ship's side to a height of 7 ft. above the keel. Forward and aft of the machinery space the protection of the inner bottom extended to a less height above the keel. It was so divided that there were four separate watertight compartments in the breadth of the vessel. Before and abaft the machinery space there was a watertight division at the centre line only, except in the foremost and aftermost tanks. Above the double bottom the vessel was constructed on the usual transverse frame system, reinforced by web frames which extended to the highest decks.

At the forward end the framing and plating was strengthened with a view to preventing panting, and damage when meeting thin harbour ice.

Beams were fitted on every frame at all decks, from the Boat deck downwards. An external bilge keel, about 300 ft. long and 25 in. deep, was fitted along the bilge amidships.

The heavy ship's plating was carried right up to the Boat deck, and between the C and B deck was doubled. The stringer or edge plate of the B deck was also doubled. This double plating was hydraulic riveted.

All decks were steel plated throughout.

The transverse strength of the ship was in part dependent on the 15 transverse watertight bulkheads, which were specially stiffened and strengthened to enable them to stand the necessary pressure in the event of accident, and they were connected by double angles to decks, inner bottom, and shell plating.

The two decks above the B deck were of comparatively light scantling, but strong enough to ensure their proving satisfactory in these positions in rough weather.

Watertight Subdivision. - In the preparation of the design of this vessel it was arranged that the bulkheads and divisions should be so placed that the ship would remain afloat in the event of any two adjoining compartments being flooded, and that they should be so built and strengthened that the ship would remain afloat under this condition. The minimum freeboard that the vessel would have, in the event of any two compartments being flooded, was between 2 ft. 6 in. and 3 ft. from the deck adjoining the top of the watertight bulkheads. With this object in view 15 watertight bulkheads were arranged in the vessel. The lower part of C bulkhead was doubled, and was in the form of a cofferdam. So far as possible the bulkheads were carried up in one plane to their upper sides, but in cases where they had for any reason to be stepped forward or aft, the deck, in way of the step, was made into a watertight flat, thus completing the watertightness of the compartment. In addition to this, G deck in the after peak was made a watertight flat. The Orlop deck between bulkheads which formed the top of the tunnel was also watertight. The Orlop deck in the forepeak tank was also a watertight flat. The electric machinery compartment was further protected by a structure some distance in from the ship's side, forming six separate watertight compartments, which were used for the storage of fresh water.

Where openings were required for the working of the ship in these watertight bulkheads they were closed by watertight sliding doors which could be worked from a position above the top of the watertight bulkhead, and those doors immediately the inner bottom were of a special automatic closing pattern, as described below. By this subdivision there were in all 73 compartments, 29 of these being above the inner bottom.

Watertight doors. - The doors (12 in number) immediately above the inner bottom were in the engine and boiler room spaces. They were of Messrs. Harland and Wolff's latest type, working vertically. The doorplate was of cast iron of heavy section, strongly ribbed. It closed by gravity, and was held in the open position by a clutch which could be released by means of a powerful electro-magnet controlled from the captain's bridge. In the event of accident, or at any time when it might be considered desirable, the captain or officer on duty could, by simply moving an electric switch, immediately close all these doors. The time required for the doors to close was between

25 and 30 seconds. Each door could also be closed from below by operating a hand lever fitted alongside the door. As a further precaution floats were provided beneath the floor level, which, in the event of water accidentally entering any of the compartments, automatically lifted and thus released the clutches, thereby permitting the doors in that particular compartment to close if they had not already been dropped by any other means. These doors were fitted with cataracts which controlled the speed of closing. Due notice of closing from the bridge was given by a warning bell.

A ladder or escape was provided in each boiler room, engine room, and similar watertight compartment, in order that the closing of the doors at any time should not imprison the men working therein.

Ship's Side Doors. - Large side doors were provided through the side plating, giving access to passengers' or crew's accommodation as follows:

On the saloon (D) deck on the starboard side in the forward third class open space one baggage door.

In way of the forward first class entrance, two doors close together on each side.

On the upper (E) deck, one door each side at the forward end of the working passage.

On the port side abreast the engine room, one door leading into the working passage. One door each side on the port and starboard sides aft into the forward second class entrance.

All the doors on the upper deck were secured by lever handles, and were made watertight by means of rubber strips. Those on the saloon deck were closed by lever handles but had no rubber.

Accommodation Ladder. - One teak accommodation ladder was provided, and could be worked on either side of the ship in the gangway way door opposite the second class entrance on the upper deck (E). It had a folding platform and portable stanchions, hand rope, etc. The ladder extended to within 3 ft. 6 in. of the vessel's light draft, and was stowed overhead in the entrance abreast the forward second class main staircase. Its lower end was arranged so as to be raised and lowered from a davit immediately above.

Masts and Rigging. - The vessel was rigged with two masts, and fore and aft sails. The two pole masts were constructed of steel, and stiffened with angle irons. The poles at the top of the mast were made of teak.

A look-out cage, constructed of steel, was fitted on the foremast at a height of about 95 ft. above the waterline. Access to the cage was obtained by an iron vertical ladder inside of the foremast, with an opening at C deck and one at the lookout cage. An iron ladder was fitted on the foremast from the hounds to the masthead light.

Life-saving Appliances

Lifebuoys. - Forty-eight, with beckets, were supplied, of pattern approved by the Board of Trade. They were placed about the ship.

Lifebelts. - 3,560 lifebelts, of the latest improved overhead pattern approved by the Board of Trade, were supplied and placed on board the vessel, and there inspected by the Board of Trade. These were distributed throughout all the sleeping accommodation.

Lifeboats. - Twenty boats in all were fitted on the vessel, and were of the following dimensions and capacities:

14 wood lifeboats, each 30 ft. long by 9 ft. 1 in. broad by 4 ft. deep, with a cubic capacity of 655·2 cubic ft., constructed to carry 65 persons each.

1 wood cutter, 25 ft. 2 in. long by 7 ft. 2 in, broad by 3 it. deep, with a cubic capacity of 326·6 cubic it., constructed to carry 40 persons.1 wood cutter, 25 ft. 2 in., long by 7 ft. 1 in. broad by 3 ft. deep, with a cubic capacity of 322·1 cubic ft., constructed to carry 40 persons.

4 Englehardt collapsible boats, 27 ft. 5 in. long by 8 ft. broad by 3 ft. deep, with a cubic capacity of 376·6 cubic ft., constructed to carry 47 persons each. Or a total of 11327·9 cubic ft. for 1,178 persons.

The lifeboats and cutters were constructed as follows:

The keels were of elm. The stems and stern posts were of oak. They were all clinker built of yellow pine, double fastened with copper nails, clinched over rooves. The timbers were of elm, spaced about 9 in. apart, and the seats pitch pine secured with galvanized iron double knees. The buoyancy tanks in the lifeboats were of 18 oz. copper, and of capacity to meet the Board of Trade requirements.

The lifeboats were fitted with Murray's disengaging gear with arrangements for simultaneously freeing both ends if required. The gear was fastened at a suitable distance from the forward and after ends of the boats, to suit the davits. Lifelines were fitted round the gunwales of the lifeboats. The davit blocks were treble for the lifeboats and double for the cutters. They were of elm, with lignum vitae roller sheaves, and were bound inside with iron, and had swivel eyes. There were manila rope falls of sufficient length for lowering the boats to the vessel's light draft, and when the boats were lowered, to be able to reach to the boat winches on the Boat deck.

The lifeboats were stowed on hinged wood chocks on the Boat deck, by groups of three at the forward, and four at the after ends. On each side of the Boat deck the cutters were arranged forward of the group of three and fitted to lash outboard as emergency boats. They were immediately abaft the navigating bridge.

The Englehardt collapsible lifeboats were stowed abreast of the cutters, one on each side of the ship, and the remaining two on top of the officers' house, immediately abaft the navigating bridge.

The boat equipment was in accordance with the Board of Trade requirements. Sails for each lifeboat and cutter were supplied and stowed in painted bags. Covers were supplied for the lifeboats and cutters, and a sea anchor for each boat. Every lifeboat was furnished with a special spirit boat compass and fitting for holding it; these compasses were carried in a locker on the Boat deck. A provision tank and water beaker were supplied to each boat.

Compasses. - Compasses were supplied as follows :

One Kelvin standard compass, with azimuth mirror on compass platform. One Kelvin steering compass inside of wheel house. One Kelvin steering compass on captain's bridge. One light card compass for docking bridge. Fourteen spirit compasses for lifeboats.

All the ship's compasses were lighted with oil and electric lamps. They were adjusted by Messrs. C. J. Smith, of Southampton, on the passage from Belfast to Southampton and Southampton to Queenstown.

Charts. - All the necessary charts were supplied.

Distress signals. - These were supplied of number and pattern approved by Board of Trade - i.e., 36 socket signals in lieu of guns, 12 ordinary rockets, 2 Manwell Holmes deck flares, 12 blue lights, and 6 lifebuoy lights.

Pumping Arrangements

The general arrangement of piping was designed so that it was possible to pump from any flooded compartment by two independent systems of 10 in. mains having cross connections between them. These were controlled from above by rods and wheels led to the level of the bulkhead deck. By these it was possible to isolate any flooded space, together with any suctions in it. If any of these should happen accidentally to be left open, and consequently out of reach, it could be shut off from the main by the wheel on the bulkhead deck. This arrangement was specially submitted to the Board of Trade and approved by them.

The double bottom of the vessel was divided by 17 transverse watertight divisions, including those bounding the fore and aft peaks, and again subdivided by a centre fore and aft bulkhead, and two longitudinal bulkheads, into 46 compartments. Fourteen of these compartments had 8 in. suctions, 23 had 6 in. suctions, and three had 5 in. suctions connected to the 10 in. ballast main suction; six compartments were used exclusively for fresh water.

The following bilge suctions were provided for dealing with water above the double bottom, viz., in No. 1 hold two 3 1/2 in. suctions, No. 2 hold two 3 1/2 in. and two 3 in. suctions, bunker hold two 3 1/2 in. and two 3 in. suctions.

The valves in connection with the forward bilge and ballast suctions were placed in the firemen's passage, the watertight pipe tunnel extending from No. 6 boiler room to the after end of No. 1 hold. In this tunnel, in addition to two 3 in. bilge suctions, one at each end, there was a special 3 1/2 in. suction with valve rod led up to the lower deck above the load line, so as always to have been accessible should the tunnel be flooded accidentally.

In No. 6 boiler room there were three 3 1/2 in., one 4 1/2 in., and two 3 in. suctions.

In No. 5 boiler room there were three 3 1/2 in., one 5 in., and two 3 in. suctions.

In No. 4 boiler room there were three 3 1/2 in., one 4 1/2 and two 3 in. suctions.

In No. 3 boiler room there were three 3 1/2 in., one 5 in., and two 3 in. suctions.

In No. 2 boiler room there were three 3 1/2 in., one 5 in., and two 3 in. suctions.

In No. 1 boiler room there were two 3 1/2 in., one 5 in., and two 3 in. suctions.

In the reciprocating engine room there were two 3 1/2 in., six 3 in., two 18 in., and two 5 in. suctions.

In the turbine engine room there were two 3 1/2 in., three 3 in., two 18 in., two 5 in., and one 4 in. suctions.

In the electric engine room there were four 3 1/2 in. suctions.

In the store rooms above the electric engine room there was one 3 in. suction.

In the forward tunnel compartment there were two 3 1/2 in. suctions.

In the watertight flat over the tunnel compartment there were two 3 in. suctions.

In the tunnel after compartment there were two 3 1/2 in. suctions.

In the watertight flat over the tunnel after compartment there were two 3 in. suctions.

Electrical Installation

Main Generating Sets. - There were four engines and dynamos, each having a capacity of 400 kilowatts at 100 volts, and consisting of a vertical three-crank compound-forced lubrication enclosed engine, of sufficient power to drive the electrical plant.

The engines were direct-coupled to their respective dynamos.

These four main sets were situated in a separate watertight compartment about 63 ft. long by 24 ft. high, adjoining the after end of the turbine room at the level of the inner bottom.

Steam to the electric engines was supplied from two separate lengths of steam pipes, connecting on the port side to the five single-ended boilers in compartment No. 1 and two in compartment No. 2, and on the starboard side to the auxiliary steam pipe which derived steam from the five single-ended boilers in No. 1 compartment, two in No. 2, and two in No. 4. By connections at the engine room forward bulkhead steam could be taken from any boiler in the ship.

Auxiliary Generating Sets. - In addition to the four main generating sets, there were two 30 kilowatt engines and dynamos situated on a platform in the turbine engine room casing on saloon deck level, 20 ft. above the waterine. They were of the same general type as the main sets.

These auxiliary emergency sets were connected to the boilers by means of a separate steam pipe running along the working passage above E deck, with branches from three boiler rooms, Nos. 2, 3 and 5, so that should the main sets be temporarily out of action the auxiliary sets could provide current for such lights and power appliances as would be required in the event of emergency.

Electric Lighting. - The total number of incandescent lights was 10,000, ranging from 16 to 100 candle power, the majority being of Tantallum type, except in the cargo spaces and for the portable fittings, where carbon lamps were provided. Special dimming lamps of small amount of light were provided in the first class rooms.

Electric Heating and Power and Mechanical Ventilation. - Altogether 562 electric heaters and 153 electric motors were installed throughout the vessel, including six 50-cwt. and two 30-cwt. cranes, four 3-ton cargo winches, and four 15-cwt. boat winches.

There were also four electric passenger lifts, three forward of the first class main entrance and one in the second class forward entrance, each to carry twelve persons.

Telephones. - Loud speaking telephones of navy pattern were fitted for communication between the following:

Wheel house on the navigating bridge and the forecastle.

Wheel house on the navigating bridge and the look-out station on the crow's-nest.

Wheel house on the navigating bridge and the engine room.

Wheel house on the navigating bridge and the poop.

Chief engineer's cabin and the engine room.

Engine room and Nos. 1, 2, 3, 4, 5 and 6 stokeholds.

These were operated both from the ship's lighting circuit, through a motor generator, and alternatively by a stand-by battery, which by means of an automatic switch could be introduced in the circuit should the main supply fail.

There was also a separate telephone system for intercommunication between a number of the chief officials and service rooms, through a 50-line exchange switchboard.

A number of the pantries and galleys were also in direct telephonic communication.

Wireless Telegraphy. - The wireless telegraphy system was worked by a Marconi 5 kilowatt motor generator. The house for the Marconi instruments was situated on the Boat deck close to the bridge. There were four parallel aerial wires extended between the masts, fastened to light booms; from the aerials the connecting wires were led to the instruments in the house. There were two complete sets of apparatus, one for transmitting and one for receiving messages, the former being in a sound-proof chamber in one corner of the wireless house.

There was also an independent storage battery and coil, in event of the failure of the current supply, which came from the ship's dynamos.

Submarine signalling. - The Submarine Signal Company's apparatus was provided for receiving signals from the submarine bells. Small tanks containing the microphones were placed on the inside of the hull of the vessel on the port and starboard sides below the water level, and were connected by wires to receivers situated in the navigating room on the port side of the officer's deck house.

Various. - The whistles were electrically actuated on the Willett Bruce system. The boiler room telegraphs, stoking indicators, rudder indicators, clocks and thermostats were also electrical. The watertight doors were released by electric magnets.

Emergency Circuit. - A separate and distinct installation was fitted in all parts of the vessel, deriving current from the two 30 kilowatt sets above mentioned, so that in the event of the current from the main dynamos being unavailable an independent supply was obtainable. Connected to the emergency circuit above were 500 incandescent lamps fitted throughout all passenger, crew and machinery compartments, at the end of passages, and near stairways, also on the Boat deck, to enable anyone to find their way from one part of the ship to the other.

The following were also connected to the emergency circuit by means of change-over switches: Five arc lamps, seven cargo and gangway lanterns, Marconi apparatus, mast, side and stern lights, and all lights on bridge, including those for captain's, navigating and chart rooms, wheel house, telegraphs and Morse signalling lanterns, and four electrically-driven boat winches. These latter, situated on the Boat deck, were each capable of lifting a load of 15 cwt. at a speed of 100 ft. per minute.

Ventilating. - There were 12 electrically driven fans for supplying air to the stokeholds; six electrically driven fans for engine and turbine room ventilation. There were fans for engine and boiler rooms.

Machinery

Description. - The propelling machinery was of the combination type, having two sets of reciprocating engines driving the wing propellers, and a low-pressure turbine working the centre propeller. Steam was supplied by 24 double-ended boilers, and 5 single-ended boilers, arranged for a working pressure of 215 lbs. per square inch. The turbine was placed in a separate compartment aft of the reciprocating engine room and divided from it by a watertight bulkhead. The main condensers, with their circulating pumps and air pumps, were placed in the turbine room. The boilers were arranged in six watertight compartments, the single-ended boilers being placed in the one nearest the main engines, the whole being built under Board of Trade survey for passenger certificate.

Reciprocating Engines. - The reciprocating engines were of the four-crank triple expansion type. Each set had four inverted, direct-acting cylinders, the high-pressure having a diameter of 54 in., the intermediate pressure of 84 in., and each of the two low-pressure cylinders of 97 in., all with a stroke of 6 ft. 3 in. The valves of the high pressure and intermediate cylinders were of the piston type, and the low-pressure cylinder had double-ported slide valves, fitted with Stephenson link motion. Each engine was reversed by a Brown's type of direct-acting steam and hydraulic engine. There was also a separate steam-driven high-pressure pump fitted for operating either or both of the reversing engines. This alternative arrangement was a stand-by in case of breakdown of the steam pipes to these engines.

Turbine. - The low-pressure turbine was of the Parson's reaction type, direct coupled to the centre line of shafting and arranged for driving in the ahead direction only. It exhausted to the two condensers, placed one on each side of it. A shut-off valve was fitted in each of the eduction pipes leading to the condensers. An emergency governor was fitted and arranged to shut off steam to the turbine and simultaneously change over the exhaust from the reciprocating engines to the condensers, should the speed of the turbine become excessive through the breaking of a shaft or other accident.

Boilers. - All the boilers were 15 ft. 9 in. in diameter, the 24 double-ended boilers being 20 ft. long, and the single-ended 11 ft. 9 in. long. Each double-ended boiler had six, and each single-ended boiler three furnaces, with a total heating surface of 144,142 sq. ft. and a grate surface of 3,466 sq. ft. The boilers were constructed in accordance with the rules of the Board of Trade for a working pressure of 215 lbs. per square inch. They were arranged for working under natural draught, assisted by fans, which blew air into the open stokehold.

Auxiliary Steam Pipes. - The five single-ended boilers and those in boiler rooms Nos. 2 and 4 had separate steam connections to the pipe supplying steam for working the auxiliary machinery, and the five single-ended boilers and the two port boilers in boiler room No. 2 had separate steam connections to the pipe supplying steam for working the electric light engines. A cross connection was also made between the main and auxiliary pipes in the reciprocating engine room, so that the auxiliaries could be worked from any boiler in the ship. Steam pipes also were led separately from three of the boiler rooms (Nos. 2, 3, 5) above the watertight bulkheads and along the working passage to the emergency electric light engines placed above the loadline in the turbine room. Pipes were also led from this steam supply to the pumps in the engine room, which were connected to the bilges throughout the ship.

Main Steam Pipes. - There were two main lines of steam pipes led to the engine room, with shut-off valves at three of the bulkheads. Besides the shut-off valves at the engine room bulkhead, a quick-acting emergency valve was fitted on each main steam pipe, so that the steam could at once be shut-off in case of rupture of the main pipe.

Condensing Plant and Pumps. - There were two main condensers, having a combined cooling surface of 50,550 square feet, designed to work under a vacuum of 28 ins. with cooling water at 60 deg. Fahr. The condensers were pear-shaped in section, and built of mild steel plates.

Four gunmetal centrifugal pumps were fitted for circulating water through the condensers. Each pump had suction and discharge pipes of 29 in. bore, and was driven by a compound engine. Besides the main sea suctions, two of the pumps had direct bilge suctions from the turbine room and the other two from the reciprocating engine room. The bilge suctions were 18 in. diameter. Four of Weir's "Dual" air pumps were fitted, two to each condenser, and discharged to two feed-tanks placed in the turbine engine room.

Bilge and Ballast Pumps. - The ship was also fitted with the following pumps: Five ballast and bilge pumps, each capable of discharging 250 tons of water per hour; three bilge pumps, each of 150 tons per hour capacity.

One ash ejector was placed in each of the large boiler compartments to work the ash ejectors, and to circulate or feed the boilers as required. This pump was also connected to the bilges, except in the case of three of the boiler rooms, where three of the ballast and bilge pumps were placed. The pumps in each case had direct bilge suctions as well as a connection to the main bilge pipe, so that each boiler room might be independent. The remainder of the auxiliary pumps were placed in the reciprocating and turbine engine rooms. Two ballast pumps were placed in the reciprocating engine room, with large suctions from the bilges direct and from the bilge main. Two bilge pumps were also arranged to draw from bilges. One bilge pump was placed in the turbine room and one of the hot salt-water pumps had a connection from the bilge main pipe for use in emergency. A 10 in. main ballast pipe was carried fore and aft through the ship with separate connections to each tank, and with filling pipes from the sea connected at intervals for trimming purposes. The five ballast pumps were arranged to draw from this pipe. A double line of bilge main pipe was fitted forward of No. 5 boiler room and aft of No. 1.

General

There were four elliptical-shaped funnels; the three forward ones took the waste gases from the boiler furnaces, and the after one was placed over the turbine hatch and was used as a ventilator. The galley funnels were led up this funnel. The uptakes by which the waste gases were conveyed to the funnels were united immediately above the watertight bulkhead which separated the boiler rooms.

All overhead discharge from the circulating pumps, ballast pumps, bilge pumps, etc., were below the deep load line, but above the light line.

The boilers were supported in built steel cradles, and were stayed to the ship's side and to each other athwart ships by strong steel stays. Built steel chocks were also fitted to prevent movement fore and aft.

Silent blow-offs from the main steam pipes were connected direct to both condensers.

Crew and Passengers

When the *Titanic* left Queenstown on 11th April the total number of persons employed on board in any capacity was 885.

The respective ratings of these persons were as follows:

Deck Department	Engine Department	Victualling Department	Total
66	325	494	885

Eight bandsmen were included in the second class passenger list.

In the Deck Department the Master, Edward Charles Smith, held an Extra Master's Certificate.

Chief Officer H. F. Wilde held an Ordinary Master's Certificate.

1st Officer W. M. Murdoch held an Ordinary Master's Certificate.

2nd Officer C. H. Lightoller held an Extra Master's Certificate.

3rd Officer H. J. Pitman held an Ordinary Master's Certificate.

4th Officer J. G. Boxhall held an Extra Master's Certificate.

5th Officer H. G. Lowe held an Ordinary Master's Certificate.

6th Officer J. P. Moody held an Ordinary Master's Certificate.

In the Engine Department were included the Chief Engineer and 7 senior and 17 assistant engineers.

In the Victualling Department there were 23 women employed.

The total number of passengers on board was 1,316.

Of these	Male	Female	Total
1st class	180	145	325
2nd class	179	106	285
3rd class	510	196	706
			1,316

Of the above, 6 children were in the 1st class, 24 were in the 2nd class, 79 were in the 3rd class, or 109 in all.

About 410 of the 3rd class passengers were foreigners, and these, with the foreigners in the 1st and 2nd class and in the Victualling Department would make a total of nearly 500 persons on board who were presumably not English speaking, so far as it is possible to ascertain. The disposition of the different classes of passengers and of the crew in the ship has already been described. In all 2,201 persons were on board.

Account of Ship's Journey across the Atlantic/Messages Received/Disaster

Sailing Orders

The Masters of vessels belonging to the White Star Line are not given any special "sailing orders" before the commencement of any particular voyage. (Ismay, 18625) It is understood, however, that the "tracks" or "lane routes" proper to the particular time of the year, and agreed upon by the great steamship companies, are to be generally adhered to. (18614-15, 18618) Should any Master see fit during this passage to deviate from his route he has to report on and explain this deviation at the end of his voyage. When such deviation has been in the interests of safety, and not merely to shorten his passage, his action has always been approved of by the Company.

A book of "General Ship's Rules and Uniform Regulations" is also issued by the Company as a guide; (18612) there are in this book no special instructions in regard to ice, but there is a general instruction that the safety of the lives of the passengers and ship are to be the first consideration. (18611-13, 18629)

Besides the book of Ship's Rules, every Master when first appointed to command a ship is addressed by special letter from the Company, of which the following passage is an extract: "You are to dismiss all idea of competitive passages with other vessels and to concentrate your attention upon a cautious, prudent and ever watchful system of navigation, which shall lose time or suffer any other temporary inconvenience rather than incur the slightest risk which can be avoided." Mr. Sanderson, one of the directors, in his evidence, says with reference to the above letter: "We never fail to tell them in handing them these letters that we do not wish them to take it as a mere matter of form; that we wish them to read these letters, and to write an acknowledgement to us that they have read them, and that they will be influenced by what we have said in those letters." (Sanderson, 19271)

Route Followed

The *Titanic* left Southampton on Wednesday, 10th April, and, after calling at Cherbourg, proceeded to Queenstown, from which port she sailed on the afternoon of Thursday, 11th April, following what was at that time the accepted outward-bound route for mail steamers from the Fastnet Light, off the southwest coast of Ireland, to the Nantucket Shoal light vessel, off the coast of the United States. It is desirable here to explain that it has been, since 1899, the practice, by common agreement between the great North Atlantic steamship companies, to follow lane routes, to be used by their ships at the different seasons of the year. Speaking generally, it may be said that the selection of these routes has hitherto been based on the importance of avoiding as much as possible the areas where fog and ice are prevalent at certain seasons, without thereby unduly lengthening the passage across the Atlantic; and also with the view of keeping the tracks of "outward" and "homeward" bound mail steamers well clear of one another. A further advantage is that, in case of a breakdown, vessels are likely to receive timely assistance from other vessels following the same route. The decisions arrived at by the steamship companies referred to above have, from time to time, been communicated to the Hydrographic Office, and the routes have there been marked on the North Atlantic route chart, printed and published by the Admiralty; and they have also been embodied in the Sailing Directions.

Before the *Titanic* disaster the accepted mail steamers outward track between January 15th and August 14th followed the arc of a great circle between the Fastnet Light and a point in latitude 42° N. and 47° W. (sometimes termed the "turning point"), and from thence by Rhumb Line so as to pass just south of the Nantucket Shoal light vessel, and from this point on to New York. This track, usually called the Outward Southern Track, was that followed by the *Titanic* on her journey.

An examination of the North Atlantic route chart shows that this track passes about 25 miles south (that is outside) of the edge of the area marked "field ice between March and July," but from 100 to 300 miles to the northward (that is inside) of the dotted line on the chart marked, "Icebergs have been seen within this line in April, May and June."

That is to say, assuming the areas indicated to be based on the experience of many years, this track might be taken as passing clear of field ice under the usual conditions of that time of year, but well inside the area in which icebergs might be seen.

It is instructive here to remark that had the "turning point" been in long 45° W. and lat. 38° N., that is some 240 miles to the southeastward, the total distance of the passage would only have been increased by about 220 miles, or some 10 hours' steaming for a 22 knot ship. This is the route which was provisionally decided on by the great Transatlantic companies subsequent to the *Titanic* disaster.

It must not be supposed that the lane routes referred to had never been changed before. Owing to the presence of ice in 1903, 1904 and 1905 from about early in April to mid-June or early in July, westward-bound vessels crossed the meridian of 47° W. in lat. 41° N., that is 60 miles further south than the then accepted track.

The publications known as "Sailing Directions," compiled by the Hydrographic Office at the Admiralty, indicate the caution which it is necessary to use in regions where ice is likely to be found.

The following is an extract from one of these books, named "United States Pilot (East Coast)," part I. (second edition, 1909, page 34), referring to the ocean passages of the large Transatlantic mail and passenger steamers:

"To these vessels, one of the chief dangers in crossing the Atlantic lies in the probability of encountering masses of ice, both in the form of bergs and of extensive fields of solid compact ice, released at the breaking up of winter in the Arctic regions, and drifted down by the Labrador Current across their direct route. Ice is more likely to be encountered to in this route between April and August, both months inclusive, than at other times, although icebergs have been seen at all seasons northward of the parallel of 43° N., but not often so far south after August.

These icebergs are sometimes over 200 ft. in height and of considerable extent. They have been seen as far south as lat. 39° N., to obtain which position they must have crossed the Gulf Stream impelled by the cold Arctic current underrunning the warm waters of the Gulf Stream. That this should happen is not to be wondered at when it is considered that the specific gravity of fresh-water ice, of which these bergs are composed, is about seven-eighths that of sea water; so that, however vast the berg may appear to the eye of the observer, he can in reality see one-eighth of its bulk, the remaining seven-eighths being submerged and subject to the deep-water currents of the ocean. The track of an iceberg is indeed directed mainly by current, so small a portion of its surface being exposed to the action of the winds that its course is but slightly retarded or deflected by moderate breezes. On the Great Bank of Newfoundland bergs are often observed to be moving south or southeast; those that drift westward of Cape Race usually pass between Green and St. Pierre Banks.

The route chart of the North Atlantic, No. 2058, shows the limits within which both field ice and icebergs may be met with, and where it should be carefully looked out for at all times, but especially during the spring and summer seasons. From this chart it would appear that whilst the southern and eastern limits of field ice are about lat. 42° N. and long. 45°

W., icebergs may be met with much farther from Newfoundland; in April, May and June they have been seen as far South as lat. 39° N., and as far east as long. 38° 30′ W."

And again on page 35:

"It is, in fact, impossible to give, within the outer limits named, any distinct idea of where ice may be expected, and no rule can be laid down to ensure safe navigation, as its position and the quantity met with differs so greatly in different seasons. Everything must depend upon the vigilance, caution and skill with which a vessel is navigated when crossing the dangerous ice-bearing regions of the Atlantic Ocean."

Similar warnings as to ice are also given in the "Nova Scotia (South-East Coast) and Bay of Fundy Pilot" (sixth edition, 1911) which is also published by the Hydrographic Office.

Both the above quoted books were supplied to the Master of the *Titanic* (together with other necessary charts and books) before that ship left Southampton.

The above extracts show that it is quite incorrect to assume that icebergs had never before been encountered or field ice observed so far south, at the particular time of year when the *Titanic* disaster occurred; but it is true to say that the field ice was certainly at that time further south than it has been seen for many years.

It may be useful here to give some definitions of the various forms of ice to be met with in these latitudes, although there is frequently some confusion in their use.

An iceberg may be defined as a detached portion of a Polar glacier carried out to sea. The ice of an iceberg formed from a glacier is of quite fresh water, only about an eighth of its mass floats above the surface of sea water.

A "Growler" is a colloquial term applied to icebergs of small mass, which therefore only show a small portion above the surface. It is not infrequently a berg which has turned over, and is therefore showing what has been termed "black ice," or more correctly, dark blue ice.

Pack Ice is the floating ice which covers wide areas of the polar seas, broken into large pieces, which are driven ("packed") together by wind and current, so as to form a practically continuous sheet. Such ice is generally frozen from seawater, and not derived from glaciers.

Field Ice is a term usually applied to frozen sea water floating in much looser form than pack ice.

An Icefloe is the term generally applied to the same ice (i.e., field ice) in a smaller quantity.

A Floe Berg is a stratified mass of floe ice (i.e., sea-water ice).

Messages Received

The *Titanic* followed the Outward Southern Track until Sunday, the 14th April, in the usual way. At 11.40 p.m. on that day she struck an iceberg and at 2.20 a.m. on the next day she foundered.

At 9 a.m. (*Titanic* time) on that day a wireless message from the S.S. *Caronia* was received by Captain Smith. It was as follows:

> "Captain, 'Titanic.' - Westbound steamers report bergs, growlers and field ice in 42° N. from 49° to 51° W., 12th April. Compliments. - Barr."

(Turnbull, 16099)

It will be noticed that this message referred to bergs, growlers and field ice sighted on the 12th April - at least 48 hours before the time of the collision. At the time this message was received the *Titanic*'s position was about lat. 43° 35' N. and long. 43° 50' W. Captain Smith acknowledged the receipt of this message.

At 1.42 p.m. a wireless message from the S.S. *Baltic* was received by Captain Smith. It was as follows:

> "Captain Smith, *Titanic*. - Have had moderate, variable winds and clear, fine weather since leaving. Greek steamer *Athenai* reports passing icebergs and large quantities of field ice to-day in lat. 41° 51' N., long. 49° 52' W. Last night we spoke German oiltank steamer *Deutschland*, Stettin to Philadelphia, not under control, short of coal, lat. 40° 42' N., long. 55° 11' W. Wishes to be reported to New York and

other steamers. Wish you and *Titanic* all success. - Commander."

(16176)

At the time this message was received the *Titanic* position was about 42° 35′ N., 45° 50′ W. Captain Smith acknowledged the receipt of this message also.

Mr. Ismay, the Managing Director of the White Star Line, was on board the *Titanic*, and it appears that the Master handed the *Baltic*'s message to Mr. Ismay almost immediately after it was received. This no doubt was in order that Mr. Ismay might know that ice was to be expected. Mr. Ismay states that he understood from the message that they would get up to the ice "that night." Mr. Ismay showed this message to two ladies, and it is therefore probable that many persons on board became aware of its contents. This message ought in my opinion to have been put on the board in the chart room as soon as it was received. It remained, however, in Mr. Ismay's possession until 7.15 p.m., when the Master asked Mr. Ismay to return it. It was then that it was first posted in the chart room.

This was considerably before the time at which the vessel reached the position recorded in the message. Nevertheless, I think it was irregular for the Master to part with the document, and improper for Mr. Ismay to retain it, but the incident had, in my opinion, no connection with or influence upon the manner in which the vessel was navigated by the Master.

It appears that about 1.45 p.m. (*Titanic* time) on the 14th a message was sent from the German steamer *Amerika* to the Hydrographic Office in Washington, which was in the following terms:

Amerika passed two large icebergs in 41° 27′ N., 50° 8′ W., on the 14th April."

(16122)

This was a position south of the point of the *Titanic*'s disaster. The message does not mention at what hour the bergs had been observed. It was a private message for the Hydrographer at Washington, but it passed to the *Titanic* because she was nearest to Cape Race, to which station it had to be sent in order to reach Washington. Being a message affecting navigation, it should in the ordinary course have been taken to the bridge. So far as can be ascertained, it was never heard of by anyone on board the *Titanic* outside the Marconi room. There were two Marconi operators in the Marconi room, namely, Phillips, who perished, and Bride, who survived and gave evidence. Bride did not receive the *Amerika* message nor did Phillips mention it to him, though the two had much conversation together after it had been received. I am of opinion that when this message reached the Marconi room it was put aside by Phillips to wait until the *Titanic* would be within call of Cape Race (at about 8 or 8.30 p.m.), and that it was never handed to any officer of the *Titanic*.

At 5.50 p.m. the *Titanic*'s course (which had been S. 62° W.) was changed to bring her on a westerly course for New York. (Boxhall, 15315) In ordinary circumstances this change in her course should have been made about half an hour earlier, but she seems on this occasion to have continued for about ten miles longer on her southwesterly course before turning, with the result that she found herself, after altering course at 5.50 p.m. about four or five miles south of the customary route on a course S. 86° W. true. Her course, as thus set, would bring her at the time of the collision to a point about two miles to the southward of the customary route and four miles south and considerably to the westward of the indicated position of the *Baltic*'s ice. Her position at the time of the collision would also be well to the southward of the indicated position of the ice mentioned in the *Caronia* message. This change of course was so insignificant that in my opinion it cannot have been made in consequence of information as to ice.

In this state of things, at 7.30 p.m. a fourth message was received, and is said by the Marconi operator Bride to have been delivered to the bridge. This message was from the S.S. *Californian* to the S.S. *Antillian*, but was picked up by the *Titanic*. It was as follows:

> "To Captain, *Antillian*, 6.30 p.m. apparent ship's time; lat. 42° 3′ N., long. 49° 9′ W. Three large bergs five miles to southward of us. Regards. - Lord."

> (Evans, 8943)

Bride does not remember to what officer he delivered this message.

By the time the *Titanic* reached the position of the collision (11.40 p.m.) she had gone about 50 miles to the westward of the indicated position of the ice mentioned in this fourth message. Thus it would appear that before the collision she had gone clear of the indicated positions of ice contained in the messages from the *Baltic* and *Californian*. As to the ice advised by the *Caronia* message, so far as it consisted of small bergs and field ice, it had before the time of the collision possibly drifted with the Gulf Stream to the eastward; and so far as it consisted of large bergs (which would be deep enough in the water to reach the Labrador current) it had probably gone to the southward. It was urged by Sir Robert Finlay, who appeared for the owners, that this is strong evidence that the *Titanic* had been carefully and successfully navigated so as to avoid the ice of which she had received warning. Mr. Ismay, however, stated that he understood from the *Baltic* message that "we would get up to the ice that night." (Ismay, 18461)

There was a fifth message received in the Marconi room of the *Titanic* at 9.40 p.m. This was from a steamer called the *Mesaba*. It was in the following terms:

> "From *Mesaba* to *Titanic* and all east-bound ships. Ice report in lat. 42° N. to 41° 25′ N., long. 49° to long. 50° 30′ W. Saw much heavy pack ice and great number large icebergs. Also field ice. Weather good, clear."

(Turnbull, 16221)

This message clearly indicated the presence of ice in the immediate vicinity of the *Titanic*, and if it had reached the bridge would perhaps have affected the navigation of the vessel. Unfortunately, it does not appear to have been delivered to the Master or to any of the officers. The Marconi operator was very busy from 8 o'clock onward transmitting messages via Cape Race for passengers on board the *Titanic*, and the probability is that he failed to grasp the significance and importance of the message, and put it aside until he should be less busy. It was never acknowledged by Captain Smith, and I am satisfied that it was not received by him. But, assuming Sir Robert Finlay's contentions to be well founded that the *Titanic* had been navigated so as to avoid the *Baltic* and the *Californian* ice, and that the *Caronia* ice had drifted to the eastward and to the southward, still there can be no doubt, if the evidence of Mr. Lightoller, the second officer, is to be believed, that both he and the

Master knew that the danger of meeting ice still existed. Mr. Lightoller says that the Master showed him the *Caronia* message about 12.45 p.m. on the 14th April when he was on the bridge. He was about to go off watch, and he says he made a rough calculation in his head which satisfied him that the *Titanic* would not reach the position mentioned in the message until he came on watch again at 6 p.m. (Lightoller 13537, 13556) At 6 p.m. Mr. Lightoller came on the bridge again to take over the ship from Mr. Wilde, the chief officer, (dead). He does not remember being told anything about the *Baltic* message, which had been received at 1.42 p.m. Mr. Lightoller then requested Mr. Moody, the sixth officer, (dead), to let him know "at what time we should reach the vicinity of ice," and says that he thinks Mr. Moody reported "about 11 o'clock." Mr. Lightoller says that 11 o'clock did not agree with a mental calculation he himself had made and which showed 9.30 as the time. This mental calculation he at first said he had made before Mr. Moody gave him 11 o'clock as the time, but later on he corrected this, and said his mental calculation was made between 7 and 8 o'clock, and after Mr. Moody had mentioned 11. He did not point out the difference to him, and thought that perhaps Mr. Moody had made his calculations on the basis of some "other" message. Mr. Lightoller excuses himself for not pointing out the difference by saying that Mr. Moody was busy at the time, probably with stellar observations. It is, however, an odd circumstance that Mr. Lightoller, who believed that the vicinity of ice would be reached before his watch ended at 10 p.m., should not have mentioned the fact to Mr. Moody, and it is also odd that if he thought that Mr. Moody was working on the basis of some "other" message, he did not ask what the other message was or where it came from. The point, however, of Mr. Lightoller's evidence is that they both thought that the vicinity of ice would be reached before midnight. When he was examined as to whether he did not fear that on entering the indicated ice region he might run foul of a growler (a low-lying berg) he answers: "No, I judged I should see it with sufficient distinctness" and at a distance of a "mile and a half, more probably two miles." He then adds:

> "In the event of meeting ice there are many things we look for. In the first place, a slight breeze. Of course, the stronger the breeze the more visible will the ice be, or, rather, the breakers on the ice."
>
> (13569)

He is then asked whether there was any breeze on this night, and he answers:

> "When I left the deck at 10 o'clock there was a slight breeze. Oh, pardon me, no; I take that back. No, it was calm, perfectly calm."

And almost immediately afterwards he describes the sea as "absolutely flat." It appeared, according to this witness, that about 9 o'clock the Master came on the bridge and that Mr. Lightoller had a conversation with him which lasted half an hour. This conversation, so far as it is material, is described by Mr. Lightoller in the following words:

> "We commenced to speak about the weather. He said, 'there is not much wind.' I said, 'No, it is a flat calm,' as a matter of fact. He repeated it, he said, 'A flat calm.' I said, 'Quite flat; there is no wind.' I said something about it was rather a pity the breeze had not kept up whilst we were going through the ice region. Of course, my reason was obvious, he knew I meant the water ripples breaking on the base of the berg. We then discussed the indications of ice. I remember saying 'In any case, there will be a certain amount of reflected light from the bergs.' He said, 'Oh, yes, there will be a certain amount of reflected light.' I said or he said - blue was said between us - that even though the blue side of the berg was towards us, probably the outline, the white outline, would give us sufficient warning, that we should be able to see it at a good distance, and as far as we could see, we should be able to see it. Of course, it was just with regard to that possibility of the blue side being towards us, and that if it did happen to be turned with the purely blue side towards us, there would still be the white outline."

Further on Mr. Lightoller says that he told the Master nothing about his own calculation as to coming up with the ice at 9.30 or about Mr. Moody's calculation as to coming up with it at 11.

The conversation with the Master ended with the Master saying, "If it becomes at all doubtful let me know at once; I will be just inside." This remark Mr. Lightoller says undoubtedly referred to ice. (13635, 13653)

At 9.30 the Master went to his room, and the first thing that Mr. Lightoller did afterwards was to send a message to the crow's nest "to keep a sharp look-out for ice, particularly small ice and growlers," until daylight. (13657) There seems to be no doubt that this message was in fact sent, and that it was passed on to the next look-outs when they came on watch. Hichens, the quartermaster, says he heard Mr. Lightoller give the message to Mr. Moody, and both the men in the crow's nest at the time (Jewell and Symons) speak to having received it. From 9.30 to 10 o'clock, when his watch ended, Mr. Lightoller remained on the bridge "looking out for ice." He also said that the night order book for the 14th had a footnote about keeping a sharp look-out for ice, and that this note was "initialled by every officer." (13700) At 10 o'clock Mr. Lightoller handed over the watch to Mr. Murdoch, the first officer, (dead), telling him that "we might be up around the ice any time now." That Mr. Murdoch knew of the danger of meeting ice appears from the evidence of Hemming, a lamp trimmer, who says that about 7.15 p.m. Mr. Murdoch told him to go forward and see the forescuttle hatch closed, "as we are in the vicinity of ice and there is a glow coming from that, and I want everything dark before the bridge." (Hemming, 17707)

The foregoing evidence establishes quite clearly that Captain Smith, the Master, Mr. Murdoch, the first officer, Mr. Lightoller, the second officer, and Mr. Moody, the sixth officer, all knew on the Sunday evening that the vessel was entering a region where ice might be expected, and this being so, it seems to me to be of little importance to consider whether the Master had by design or otherwise succeeded in avoiding the particular ice indicated in the three messages received by him.

Speed of the Ship

The entire passage had been made at high speed, though not at the ship's maximum, and this speed was never reduced until the collision was unavoidable. At 10 p.m. the ship was registering 45 knots every two hours by the Cherub log. (Hichens, 965)

The quartermaster on watch aft, when the *Titanic* struck, states that the log, reset at noon, then registered 260 knots, (Rowe, 17608) and the fourth officer, when working up the position from 7.30 p.m. to the time of the collision, states he estimated the *Titanic*'s speed as 22 knots, (Boxhall, 15645) and this is also borne out by evidence that the engines were running continuously at 75 revolutions.

Weather Conditions

From 6 p.m. onwards to the time of the collision the weather was perfectly clear and fine. (Lightoller, 13616) There was no moon, the stars were out, and there was not a cloud in the sky. There was, however, a drop in temperature of 10 deg. in slightly less than two hours, and by about 7.30 p.m. the temperature was 33 deg. F., and it eventually fell to 32 deg. F. That this was not necessarily an indication of ice is borne out by the Sailing Directions. The Nova Scotia (S.E. Coast) and Bay of Fundy Pilot (6th edition, 1911, page 16) says:

> "No reliance can be placed on any warning being conveyed to a mariner by a fall of temperature either of the air or sea, on approaching ice. Some decrease in temperature has occasionally been recorded, but more often none has been observed."

Sir Ernest Shackleton was, however, of opinion that "if there was no wind and the temperature fell abnormally for the time of the year, I would consider that I was approaching an area which might have ice in it." (Shackleton, 25062)

Action That Should Have Been taken

The question is what ought the Master to have done. I am advised that with the knowledge of the proximity of ice which the Master had, two courses were open to him: The one was to stand well to the southward instead of turning up to a westerly course; the other was to reduce speed materially as night approached. He did neither. The alteration of the course at 5.50 p.m. was so insignificant that it cannot be attributed to any intention to avoid ice. This deviation brought the vessel back to within about two miles of the customary route before 11.30 p.m. And there was certainly no reduction of speed. Why, then, did the Master persevere in his course and maintain his speed? The answer is to be found in the evidence. It was shown that for many years past, indeed, for a quarter of a century or more, the practice of liners using this track when in the vicinity of ice at night had been in clear weather to keep the course, to maintain the speed and to trust to a sharp look-out to enable them to avoid the danger. This practice, it was said, had been justified by experience, no casualties having resulted from it. I accept the evidence as to the practice and as to the immunity from casualties which is said to have accompanied it. But the event has proved the practice to be bad. Its root is probably to be found in competition and in the desire of the public for quick passages rather than in the judgment of navigators. But unfortunately experience appeared to justify it. In these circumstances I am not able to blame Captain Smith. He had not the experience which his own misfortune has afforded to those whom he has left behind, and he was doing only that which other skilled men would have done in the same position. It was suggested at the bar that he was yielding to influences which ought not to have affected him; that the presence of Mr. Ismay on board and the knowledge which he perhaps had of a conversation between Mr. Ismay and the Chief Engineer at Queenstown about the speed of the ship and the consumption of coal probably induced him to neglect precautions which he would otherwise have taken. But I do not believe this. The evidence shows that he was not trying to make any record passage or indeed any exceptionally quick passage. He was not trying to please anybody, but was exercising his own discretion in the way he thought best. He made a mistake, a very grievous mistake, but one in which, in face of the practice and of past experience, negligence cannot he said to have had any part; and in the absence of negligence it is, in my opinion, impossible to fix Captain Smith with blame. It is, however, to be hoped that the last has been heard of the practice and that for the future it will be abandoned for what we now know to be more prudent and wiser measures. What was a mistake in the case of the *Titanic* would without doubt be negligence in any similar case in the future.

The Collision

Mr. Lightoller turned over the ship to Mr. Murdoch, the first officer, at 10 o'clock, telling him that the ship was within the region where ice had been reported. (Lightoller, 13710) He also told him of the message he had sent to the crow's nest, and of his conversation with the Master, and of the latter's orders. (13720)

The ship appears to have run on, on the same course, until, at a little before 11.40, one of the look-outs in the crow's nest struck three blows on the gong, (Hichens, 969) which was the accepted warning for something ahead, following this immediately afterwards by a telephone message to the bridge "Iceberg right ahead." Almost simultaneously with the three gong signal Mr. Murdoch, the officer of

The White Star Line began construction of the *Titanic* in 1909.

Unable to match competing liners like *Lusitania* in speed, *Titanic* opted for luxury and splendor instead.

Titanic leaves England for her maiden voyage.

Captain Edward John Smith. One of the White Star Line's most experienced captains, he was to retire after *Titanic's* trip to New York.

A contemporary illustration shows the *Titanic's* last moments.

The passenger liner *Carpathia* heard *Titanic's* radio calls for help and raced towards her position. This was the view from *Carpathia* of the ice field.

When *Carpathia* arrived at *Titanic*'s position, nothing remained but the lifeboats.

Survivors from *Titanic's* lifeboats are taken aboard *Carpathia*. Although *Titanic* carried more lifeboats than required by British maritime law, there still were not enough for all the passengers.

Titanic survivors huddling on the deck of *Carpathia*.

Carpathia enters New York Harbor with *Titanic's* lifeboats on her deck.

The White Star Office in New York on April 15. Although White Star attempted to get *Titanic*'s crew back to England on the next available ship, the US Senate was able to serve notices for surviving crew to testify at its inquest.

J. Bruce Ismay, Chairman of the White Star Line and a survivor of the *Titanic*, testifies before the US Senate inquiry.

Lord Mersey, who presided over the official British inquiry into the *Titanic* disaster.

Hearings during the British Wreck Commission's inquiry.

the watch, gave the order "Hard-a-starboard," and immediately telegraphed down to the engine room "Stop. Full speed astern." (Boxhall, 15346) The helm was already "hard over," and the ship's head had fallen off about two points to port, when she collided with an iceberg well forward on her starboard side.

Mr. Murdoch at the same time pulled the lever over which closed the watertight doors in the engine and boiler rooms. (15352)

The Master "rushed out" on to the bridge and asked Mr. Murdoch what the ship had struck. (Hichens, 1027) (Boxhall, 15353)

Mr. Murdoch replied: "An iceberg, Sir. I hard-a-starboarded and reversed the engines, and I was going to hard-a-port round it but she was too close. I could not do any more. I have closed the watertight doors." (15355)

From the evidence given it appears that the *Titanic* had turned about two points to port before the collision occurred. From various experiments subsequently made with the S.S. *Olympic*, a sister ship to the *Titanic*, it was found that travelling at the same rate as the *Titanic*, about 37 seconds would be required for the ship to change her course to this extent after the helm had been put hard-a-starboard. In this time the ship would travel about 466 yards, and allowing for the few seconds that would be necessary for the order to be given, it may be assumed that 500 yards was about the distance at which the iceberg was sighted either from the bridge or crow's-nest.

That it was quite possible on this night, even with a sharp lookout at the stemhead, crow's nest and on the bridge, not to see an iceberg at this distance is shown by the evidence of Captain Rostron, of the *Carpathia*. (Rostron, 25401)

The injuries to the ship, which are described in the next section, were of such a kind that she foundered in two hours and forty minutes.

Description of the Damage to the Ship and its Gradual Final Effect

Extent of the Damage

The collision with the iceberg, which took place at 11.40 p.m., caused damage to the bottom of the starboard side of the vessel at about 10 feet above the level the keel, but there was no damage above this height. There was damage in: The forepeak, No. 1 hold, No. 2 hold, No. 3 hold, No. 6 boiler room, No. 5 boiler room.

The damage extended over a length of about 300 ft.

Time in which the damage was done

As the ship was moving at over 20 knots, she would have passed through 300 ft. in less than 10 seconds, so that the damage was done in about this time.

Flooding in the First Ten Minutes

At first it is desirable to consider what happened in the first 10 minutes.

The forepeak was not flooded above the Orlop deck - i.e., the peak tank top, from the hole in the bottom of the peak tank.

In No. 1 hold there was 7 ft. of water. (Poingdestre, 2821-2)

In No. 2 hold five minutes after the collision water was seen rushing in at the bottom of the firemen's passage on the starboard side, (Hendrickson, 4859) so that the ship's side was damaged abaft of bulkhead B sufficiently to open the side of the firemen's passage, which was 3 1/2 ft. from the outer skin of the ship, thereby flooding both the hold and the passage. (4856-66, 70)

In No. 3 hold the mail room was filled soon after the collision. The floor of the mail room is 24 ft. above the keel.

In No. 6 boiler room, when the collision took place, water at once poured in at about 2 feet above the stokehold plates, on the starboard side, at the after end of the boiler room. (Barrett, 1868-74) Some of the firemen immediately went through the watertight door opening to No. 5 boiler room because the water was flooding the place. (1899, 1905) The watertight doors in the engine rooms were shut from the bridge almost immediately after the collision. Ten minutes later it was found that there was water to the height of 8 feet above the double bottom in No. 6 boiler room. (1937, 1926)

No. 5 boiler room was damaged at the ship's side in the starboard forward bunker (1917) at a distance of 2 feet above the stokehold plates, (1921) at 2 feet from the watertight bulkhead between Nos. 5 and 6 boiler rooms. (2105) Water poured in at that place as it would from an ordinary fire hose. (2255) At the time of the collision this bunker had no coal in it. (2091) The bunker door was closed when water was seen to be entering the ship. (2343)

In No. 4 boiler room there was no indication of any damage at the early stages of the sinking.

Gradual Effect of the Damage

It will thus be seen that all the six compartments forward of No. 4 boiler room were open to the sea by damage which existed at about 10 feet above the keel. At 10 minutes after the collision the water seems to have risen to about 14 feet above the keel in all these compartments except No. 5 boiler room. After the first ten minutes, the water rose steadily in all these six compartments. The forepeak above the peak tank was not filled until an hour after the collision when the vessel's bow was submerged to above C deck. The water then flowed in from the top through the deck scuttle forward of the collision bulkhead. It was by this scuttle that access was obtained to all the decks below C down to the peak tank top on the Orlop deck.

At 12 o'clock water was coming up in No. 1 hatch. (Lee, 2455, 79) It was getting into the firemen's quarters and driving the firemen out. (2485) It was rushing round No. 1 hatch on G deck and coming mostly from the starboard side, so that in 20 minutes the water had risen above G deck in No. 1 hold. (Pitman, 14962, 65)

In No. 2 hold about 40 minutes after the collision the water was coming in to the seamen's quarters on E deck through a burst fore and aft wooden bulkhead of a third class cabin opposite the seamen's wash place. (Poingdestre, 2844-45) Thus, the water had risen in No. 2 hold to about 3 ft. above E deck in 40 minutes.

In No. 3 hold the mail room was afloat about 20 minutes after the collision. The bottom of the mail room which is on the Orlop deck, is 24 feet above the keel. (Pitman, 14948-49)

The watertight doors on F deck at the fore and after ends of No. 3 compartment were not closed then. (Boxhall, 15757)

The mail room was filling and water was within 2 ft. of G deck, rising fast, when the order was given to clear the boats. (15374, 80) (Johnson, 3397)

There was then no water on F deck.

There is a stairway on the port side on G deck which leads down to the first class baggage room on the Orlop deck immediately below. There was water in this baggage room 25 minutes after the collision. Half an hour after the collision water was up to G deck in the mail room.

Thus the water had risen in this compartment to within 2 ft. of G deck in 20 minutes, and above G deck in 25 to 30 minutes.

No. 6 boiler room was abandoned by the men almost immediately after the collision. Ten minutes later the water had risen to 8 ft. above the top of the double bottom, and probably reached the top of the bulkhead at the after end of the compartment, at the level of E deck, in about one hour after the collision.

In No. 5 boiler room there was no water above the stokehold plates, until a rush of water came through the pass between the boilers from the forward end, and drove the leading stoker out. (Barrett, 1969)

It has already been shown in the description of what happened in the first ten minutes, that water was coming into No. 5 boiler room in the forward starboard bunker at 2 ft. above the plates in a stream about the size of a deck hose. The door in this bunker had been dropped probably when water was first discovered, which was a few minutes after the collision. This would cause the water to be retained in the bunker until it rose high enough to burst the door which was weaker than the bunker bulkhead. This happened about an hour after the collision. (2038, 39, 41)

No. 4 boiler room. - One hour and 40 minutes after collision water was coming in forward, in No. 4 boiler room, from underneath the floor in the forward part, in small quantities. The men remained in that stokehold till ordered on deck.

Nos. 3, 2 and 1 boiler rooms. - When the men left No. 4 some of them went through Nos. 3, 2 and 1 boiler rooms into the reciprocating engine room, and from there on deck. (Dillon, 3795) There was no water in the boiler rooms abaft No. 4 one hour 40 minutes after the collision (1.20 a.m.), (3811) and there was then none in the reciprocating and turbine engine rooms.

Electrical engine room and tunnels. - There was no damage to these compartments.

From the foregoing it follows that there was no damage abaft No. 4 boiler room.

All the watertight doors aft of the main engine room were opened after the collision. (Scott, 5599)

Half an hour after the collision the watertight doors from the engine room to the stokehold were opened as far forward as they could be to No. 4 boiler room.

Final Effect of the Damage

The later stages of the sinking cannot be stated with any precision, owing to a confusion of the times which was natural under the circumstances.

The forecastle deck was not under water at 1.35 a.m. (Lee, 2541) Distress signals were fired until two hours after the collision (1.45 a.m.). (Rowe, 17685) At this time the fore deck was under water. (Jewell, 167) The forecastle head was not then submerged though it was getting close down to the water, about half an hour before she disappeared (1.50 a.m.). (Lightoller, 14081)

When the last boat, lowered from davits (D), left the ship, A deck was under water, (14023) and water came up the stairway under the Boat deck almost immediately afterwards. After this the other port collapsible (B), which had been stowed on the officers' house, was uncovered, the lashings cut adrift, and she was swung round over the edge of the coamings of the deckhouse on to the Boat deck. (14035)

Very shortly afterwards the vessel, according to Mr. Lightoller's account, seemed to take a dive, and he just walked into the water. (14052) When he came to the surface all the funnels were above the water. (14071-72)

Her stern was gradually rising out of the water, and the propellers were clear of the water. (14078) The ship did not break in two; (14075) [today we know that the *Titanic* did in fact break in two, just before sinking – Editor] and she did eventually attain the perpendicular, (14084a) when the second funnel from aft about reached the water. (14089) There were no lights burning then, though they kept alight practically until the last. (Lee, 2558) (Pearcey, 10454)

Before reaching the perpendicular when at an angle of 50 or 60 degrees, there was a rumbling sound which may be attributed to the boilers leaving their beds and crashing down on to or through the bulkheads. (Lightoller, 14097) She became more perpendicular and finally absolutely perpendicular, when she went slowly down.

After sinking as far as the after part of the Boat deck she went down more quickly. The ship disappeared at 2.20 a.m. (Lee, 2558)

Observations

I am advised that the *Titanic* as constructed could not have remained afloat long with such damage as she received. Her bulkheads were spaced to enable her to remain afloat with any two compartments in communication with the sea. She had a sufficient margin of safety with any two of the compartments flooded which were actually damaged. (Wilding, 20286, 93)

In fact any three of the four forward compartments could have been flooded by the damage received without sinking the ship to the top of her bulkheads. (20364)

Even if the four forward compartments had been flooded the water would not have got into any of the compartments abaft of them though it would have been above the top of some of the forward bulkheads. But the ship, even with these four compartments flooded would have remained afloat. But she could not remain afloat with the four forward compartments and the forward boiler room (No. 6) also flooded.

The flooding of these five compartments alone would have sunk the ship sufficiently deeply to have caused the water to rise above the bulkhead at the after end of the forward boiler room (No. 6) and to flow over into the next boiler room (No. 5), and to fill it up until in turn its after bulkhead would be overwhelmed and the water would thereby flow over and fill No. 4 boiler room, and so on in succession to the other boiler rooms till the ship would ultimately fill and sink.

It has been shown that water came into the five forward compartments to a height of about 14 feet above the keel in the first ten minutes. This was at a rate of inflow with which the ship's pumps could not possibly have coped, so that the damage done to these five compartments alone inevitably sealed the doom of the ship.

The damage done in the boiler rooms Nos. 5 and 4 was too slight to have hastened appreciably the sinking of the ship, for it was given in evidence that no considerable amount of water was in either of these compartments for an hour after the collision. The rate at which water came into No. 6 boiler room makes it highly probable that the compartment was filled in not more than an hour, after which the flow over the top of the bulkhead between 5 and 6 began and continued till No. 5 was filled.

It was shown that the leak in No. 5 boiler room was only about equal to the flow of a deck hose pipe about 3 inches in diameter. (Barrett, 2255)

The leak in No. 4, supposing that there was one, was only enough to admit about 3 feet of water in that compartment in 1 hour 40 minutes. (Cavell, 4265) (Dillon, 3811)

Hence the leaks in Nos. 4 and 5 boiler rooms did not appreciably hasten the sinking of the vessel.

The evidence is very doubtful as to No. 4 being damaged. The pumps were being worked in No. 5 soon after the collision. (Barrett, 1961) The 10 inch leather special suction pipe which was carried from aft is more likely to have been carried for use in No. 5 than No. 4 because the doors were ordered to be opened probably soon after the collision when water was known to be coming into No. 5. There is no evidence that the pumps were being worked in No. 4.

The only evidence possibly favourable to the view that the pipe was required for No. 4, and not for No. 5, is that Scott, a greaser, says that he saw engineers dragging the suction pipe along 1 hour after the collision. But even as late as this it may have been wanted for No. 5 only. (Scott, 5602)

The importance of the question of the damage to No. 5 is small because the ship, as actually constructed, was doomed as soon as the water in No. 6 boiler room and all compartments forward of it entered in the quantities it actually did. (Wilding, 20311-4, 20320, 20355)

It is only of importance in dealing with the question of what would have happened to the ship had she been more completely subdivided.

It was stated in evidence that if No. 4 had not been damaged or had only been damaged to an extent within the powers of the pumps to keep under, then, if the bulkheads had been carried to C deck, the ship might have been saved. (20371-4) Further methods of increased subdivision and their effect upon the fate of the ship are discussed later.

Evidence was given showing that after the watertight doors in the engine and boiler rooms had been all closed, except those forward of No. 4 group of boilers, they were opened again, (Dillon, 3738, 3745, 3770) and there is no evidence to show that they were again closed. Though it is probable that the engineers who remained below would have closed these doors as the water rose in the compartments, yet it was not necessary for them to do this as each door had an automatic closing arrangement which would have come into operation immediately had a small amount of water came through the door.

It is probable, however, that the life of the ship would have been lengthened somewhat if these doors had been left open, for the water would have flowed through them to the after part of the ship, and the rate of flow of the water into the ship would have been for a time reduced as the bow might have been kept up a little by the water which flowed aft.

It is thus seen that the efficiency of the automatic arrangements for the closing of the watertight doors, which was questioned during the enquiry, had no important bearing on the question of hastening the sinking of the ship, except that, in the case of the doors not having been closed by the engineers, it might have retarded the sinking of the ship if they had not acted. The engineers would not have prevented the doors from closing unless they had been convinced that the ship was doomed. There is no evidence that they did prevent the doors from closing.

The engineers were applying the pumps when Barrett, leading stoker, left No. 5 boiler room, but even if they had succeeded in getting all the pumps in the ship to work they could not have saved the ship or prolonged her life to any appreciable extent.

Effect of Additional Subdivision on Flotation

Watertight decks. - It is in evidence that advantage might be obtained from the point of view of greater safety in having a watertight deck. (Archer, 24424)

Without entering into the general question of the advantage of watertight decks for all ships, it is desirable to form an opinion in the case of the *Titanic* as to whether making the bulkhead deck watertight would have been an advantage in the circumstances of the accident, or in case of accident to ships of this class.

I am advised that it is found that with all the compartments certainly known to have been flooded, viz., those forward of No. 4 boiler room, the ship would have remained afloat if the bulkhead deck had been a watertight deck. If, however, No. 4 boiler room had also been flooded the ship would not have remained afloat unless, in addition to making the bulkhead deck watertight, the transverse bulkhead abaft of No. 4 boiler room had been carried up to D deck.

To make the bulkhead deck effectively watertight for this purpose it would have been necessary to carry watertight trunks round all the openings in the bulkhead deck up to C deck.

It has been shown that with the bulkhead abaft No. 5 boiler room carried to C deck the ship would have remained afloat if the compartments certainly known to have been damaged had been flooded. (Scarrott, 518)

I do not desire to express an opinion upon the question whether it would have conduced to safety in the case of the *Titanic* if a watertight deck had been fitted below the water line, as there may be some objections to such a deck. (Archer, 24426) There are many considerations involved, and I think that the matter should be dealt with by the Bulkhead Committee for ships in general.

Longitudinal Subdivision. - The advantages and disadvantages of longitudinal subdivision by means of watertight bunker bulkheads were pointed out in evidence. (Wilding, 20209-37, 20284-98, 25297-8)

While not attempting to deal with this question generally for ships, I am advised that if the *Titanic* had been divided in the longitudinal method, instead of in the transverse method only, she would have been able, if damaged as supposed, to remain afloat, though with a list which could have been corrected by putting water ballast into suitable places.

This subject is one, however, which again involves many considerations, and I think that for ships generally the matter should be referred to the Bulkhead Committee for their consideration and report.

Extending double bottom up the sides. - It was shown in evidence that there would be increased protection in carrying the double bottom higher up the side than was done in the *Titanic*, and that some of the boiler rooms would probably not then have been flooded, as water could not have entered the ship except in the double bottom. (20350-1)

In the case of the *Titanic* I am advised that this would have been an advantage, but it was pointed out in evidence that there are certain disadvantages which in some ships may outweigh the advantages.

In view of what has already been said about the possible advantages of longitudinal subdivision, it is unnecessary further to discuss the question of carrying up the double bottom in ships generally. This matter should also be dealt with by the Bulkhead Committee.

Watertight doors. - With reference to the question of the watertight doors of the ship, there does not appear to have been any appreciable effect upon the sinking of the ship caused by either shutting or not shutting the doors. There does not appear to have been any difficulty in working the watertight doors. They appear to have been shut in good time after the collision.

But in other cases of damage in ships constructed like the *Titanic*, it is probable that the efficiency of the closing arrangement of the watertight doors may exert a vital influence on the safety of the ship. It has been represented that in the future consideration should be given to the question "as to how far bulkheads should be solid bulkheads, and how far there should be watertight doors, and, if there should be watertight doors, how far they may or may not be automatically operated." This again is a question on which it is not necessary here to express any general opinion, for there are conflicting considerations which vary in individual cases. The matter, however, should come under the effective supervision of the Board of Trade much more than it seems to come at present, and should be referred to the Bulkhead Committee for their consideration with a view to their suggesting in detail where doors should or should not be allowed, and the type of door which should be adopted in the different parts of ships.

Account of the Saving and Rescue of Those Who Survived

Boats

The *Titanic* was provided with 20 boats. They were all on the Boat deck. Fourteen were lifeboats. These were hung inboard in davits, seven on the starboard side and seven on the port side, and were designed to carry 65 persons each. Two were emergency boats. These were also in davits, but were hung outboard, one on the starboard side and one on the port side, and were designed to carry 40 persons each. The remaining four boats were Englehardt or collapsible boats. (Sanderson, 19115-22) Two of these were stowed on the Boat deck and two on the roof of the officers' quarters, and were designed carry 47 persons each. Thus the total boat accommodation was 1,178 persons. The boats in davits were numbered, the odd numbers being on the starboard side and even numbers on the port side. The numbering began with emergency boats which were forward, and ran aft. Thus the boats on the starboard side were numbered 1 (an emergency boat) 3, 5, 7, 9, 11, 13 and 15 (lifeboats), and those on the port side 2 (an emergency boat), 4, 6, 8, 10, 12, 14 and 16 (lifeboats). The collapsible boats were lettered, A and B being on the roof of the officers' quarters, and C and D being on the Boat deck; C was abreast of No. 1 (emergency boat) and D abreast of No. 2 (emergency boat). Further particulars as to the boats will be found elswhere.

In ordinary circumstances all these boats (with the exception of 1 and 2) were kept covered up, and contained only a portion of their equipment, such as oars, masts and sails, and water; some of the remaining portion, such as lamps, compasses and biscuits being stowed in the ship in some convenient place, ready for use when required. Much examination was directed at the hearing to show that some boats left the ship without a lamp and others without a compass and so on, but in the circumstances of confusion and excitement which existed at the time of the disaster this seems to me to be excusable.

Each member of the crew had a boat assigned to him in printed lists which were posted up in convenient places for the men to see; but it appeared that in some cases the men had not looked at these lists and did not know their respective boats.

There had been no proper boat drill nor a muster. It was explained that great difficulty frequently exists in getting firemen to take part in a boat drill. They regard it as no part of their work. There seem to be no statutory requirements as to boat drills or musters, although there is a provision (Section 9 of the Merchant Shipping Act of 1906) that when a boat drill does take place the Master of the vessel is, under a penalty, to record the fact in his log. I think it is desirable that the Board of Trade should make rules requiring boat drills and boat musters to be held of such a kind and at such times as may be suitable to the ship and to the voyage on which she is engaged. Boat drill, regulated according to the opportunities of the service, should always be held.

It is perhaps worth recording that there was an inspection of the boats themselves at Southampton by Mr. Clarke, the emigration officer; and that, as a result, Mr. Clarke gave his certificate that the boats were satisfactory. For the purpose of this inspection two of the boats were lowered to the water and crews exercised in them. (Clarke, 24096-103)

The collision took place at 11.40 p.m. (ship's time). About midnight it was realized that that the vessel could not live, and at about 12.50 the order was given to uncover the 14 boats under davits. (Boxhall, 15367) The work began on both sides of the ship under the superintendence of five officers. (Lightoller, 13800) It did not proceed quickly at first; the crew arrived on the Boat deck only gradually, and there was an average of not more than three deck hands to each boat. (13809) At 12.20 the order was given to swing out the boats, and this work was at once commenced. There were a few passengers on the deck at this time. Mr. Lightoller, who was one of the officers directing operations, says that the noise of the steam blowing off was so great that his voice could not be heard, and that he had to give directions with his hands. (Lightoller, 13811) (Hart, 9926, 9879) (Wheat, 10943, 13229)

Before this work had been begun, the stewards were rousing the passengers in their different quarters, helping them to put on lifebelts and getting them up to the Boat deck. At about 12.30 the order was given to place women and children in the boats. This was proceeded with at once and at about 12.45 Mr. Murdoch gave the order to lower No. 7 boat (on the starboard side) to the water. The work of uncovering, filling and lowering the boats was done under the following supervision: Mr. Lowe, the fifth officer, saw to Nos. 1, 3, 5 and 7; Mr. Murdoch (lost) saw also to 1 and 7 and to A and C. Mr. Moody (lost) looked after Nos. 9, 11, 13 and 15. Mr. Murdoch also saw to 9 and 11. Mr. Lightoller saw to Nos. 4, 6, 8, B and D. Mr. Wilde (lost) also saw to 8 and D. Mr. Lightoller and Mr. Moody saw to 10 and 16 and Mr. Lowe to 12 and 14. Mr. Wilde also assisted at No. 14, Mr. Boxhall helping generally. (Various Witnesses, 15809, 14987, 14048, 10393, 13326, 708, 13187, 13835, 13931, 14011, 13929, 13984, 13819, 15832, 2969, 383, 16526, 17926)

The evidence satisfies me that the officers did their work very well and without any thought of themselves. Captain Smith, the Master, Mr. Wilde, the chief officer, Mr. Murdoch, the first officer, and Mr. Moody, the sixth officer, all went down with the ship while performing their duties. The others, with the exception of Mr. Lightoller, took charge of boats and thus were saved. Mr. Lightoller was swept off the deck as the vessel went down and was subsequently picked up.

So far as can be ascertained the boats left the ship at the following times, but I think it is necessary to say that these, and, indeed, all the times subsequent to the collision which are mentioned by the witnesses, are unreliable.

No.	Starboard Side.	No.	Port Side.
7	At 12.45 a.m.	6	At 12.55 a.m.
5	12.55 a.m.	8	1.10
3	1.0	10	1.20
1	1.10	12	1.25
9	1.20	14	1.30
11	1.25	16	1.35
13	1.35	2	1.45
15	1.35	4	1.55
C	1.40	D	2.15
A	Floated off when the ship sank and was utilised as a raft.	B	Floated off when the ship sank and was utilised as a raft.

As regards the collapsible boats, C and D were properly lowered; as to A and B, which were on the roof of the officer's house, they were left until the last. There was difficulty in getting these boats down to the deck, and the ship had at this time a list. Very few of the deck hands were left in the ship, as they had nearly all gone to man the lifeboats, and the stewards and firemen were unaccustomed to work the collapsible boats. Work appears to been going on in connection with these two boats at the time that the ship sank. The boats seem to have floated from the deck and to have served in the water as rafts. (Brown, 10530) (Lightoller, 14011, 14035)

The following table shows the numbers of the male crew, male passengers, and women and children who, according to the evidence, left the ship in each boat. In three or four instances the numbers of women and children are only arrived at by subtracting the numbers of crew and male passengers from the total said to be in the boat (these are in italics). In each case the lowest figures are taken:

Starboard side Boat No.	Men of crew	Men Passengers	Women and Children	Total	Port side Boat No.	Men of crew.	Men Passengers	Women and Children	Total
7	3	4	20	27	6	2	2	24	28
5	5	6	30	41	8	4	-	35	39
3	15	10	25	50	10	5	-	50	55
1	7	8	2	12	2	4	1	21	26
9	8	6	42	56	12	2	-	40	42
11	9	1	60	70	14	8	2	53	63
13	5	-	59	64	16	6	-	50	56
15	13	4	53	70	4	4	-	36	40
C	5	2	64	71	D	2	2	40	44
A	Utilised after the ship sank.				B	Utilised after the ship sank.			
Totals	70	36	355	461	Totals	37	7	349	393

General Total:

107 men of the crew
43 men passengers
704 women and children

This shows in all 107 men the crew, 43 male passengers, and 704 women and children, or a total of 854 in 18 boats. In addition, about 60 persons, two of whom were women, were said to have been transferred, subsequently, from A and B collapsible boats to other boats, were rescued from the water, making a total of 914 who escaped with their lives. It is obvious that these figures are quite unreliable, for only 712 were, in fact, saved by the *Carpathia*, the steamer which came to the rescue at about 4 a.m., and all the boats were accounted for. Another remarkable discrepancy is that, of the 712 saved, 189 were, in fact, men of the crew, 129 were male passengers and 394 were women and children. In other words, the real proportion of women to men saved was much less than the proportion appearing in the evidence from the boats. Allowing for those subsequently picked up, of the 712 persons saved only 652 could have left the *Titanic* in boats, or an average of about 36 per boat. There was a tendency in the evidence to exaggerate the numbers in each boat, to exaggerate the proportion of women to men, and to diminish the number of crew. I do not attribute this to any wish on the part of the witnesses to mislead the Court, but to a natural desire to make the best case for themselves and their ship. The seamen who gave evidence were too frequently encouraged when under examination in the witness-box to understate the number of crew in the boats. The number of crew actually saved was 189, giving an average of 10 per boat; and if from this figure the 58 men of the 60 persons above mentioned be deducted the average number of crew leaving the ship in the boats must still have been at least 7. The probability, however, is that many of the 60 picked up were passengers.

The discipline both among passengers and crew during the lowering of the boats was good, but the organisation should have been better, and if it had been it is possible that more lives would have been saved. (Various Witnesses, 104, 723, 14006, 1504, 6448)

The real difficulty in dealing with the question of the boats is to find the explanation of so many of them leaving the ship with comparatively few persons in them. No. 1 certainly left with only 12; this was an emergency boat with a carrying capacity of 40. No. 7 left with only 27, and No. 6 with only 28; these were lifeboats with a carrying capacity of 65 each; and several of the others, according to the evidence and certainly according to the truth, must have left only partly filled. Many explanations are forthcoming, one being that the passengers were unwilling to leave the ship. (Various Witnesses, 1127, 1146, 5955, 13996, 15931, 9924, 25566) When the earlier boats left, and before the *Titanic* had begun materially to settle down, there was a drop of 65 feet from the Boat deck to the water, and the women feared to get into the boats. Many people thought that the risk in the ship was less than the risk in the boats. This explanation is supported by the evidence of Captain Rostron, of the *Carpathia*. He says that after those who were saved got on board his ship, he was told by some of them that when the boats first left the *Titanic* the people "really would not be put in the boats; they did not want to go in." There was a large body of evidence from the *Titanic* to the same effect, and I have no doubt that many people, particularly women, refused to leave the deck for the boats. At one time the Master appears to have had the intention of putting the people into the boats from the gangway doors in the side of the ship. This was possibly with a view to allay the fears of the passengers, for from these doors the water could be reached by means of ladders, and the lowering of some of the earlier boats when only partly filled may be accounted for in this way. There is no doubt that the Master did order some of the partly filled boats to row to a position under one of the doors with the object taking in passengers at that point. It appears, however, that these doors were never opened. Another explanation is that some women refused to leave their husbands. It is said further that the officers engaged in putting the people into the boats feared that the boats might buckle if they were filled; but this proved to be an unfounded apprehension, for one or more boats were completely filled and then successfully lowered to the water. (Various Witnesses, 13887, 13954, 16011, 17897, 2156)

At 12.35 the message from the *Carpathia* was received announcing that she was making for the *Titanic*. (Bride, 16798) This probably became known and may have tended to make the passengers still more unwilling to leave the ship; and the lights of a ship (the *Californian*) which were seen by many people may have encouraged the passengers to hope that assistance was at hand. These explanations are perhaps sufficient to account for so many of the lifeboats leaving without a full boat load; but I think, nevertheless, that if the boats had been kept a little longer before being lowered, or if the after gangway doors had been opened, more passengers might have been induced to enter the boats. And if women could not be induced to enter the boats, the boats ought to then to have been filled up with men. It is difficult to account for so many of the lifeboats being sent from the sinking ship, in a smooth sea, far from full. These boats left behind them many hundreds of lives to perish. I do not, however, desire these observations to be read as casting any reflection on the officers of the ship or on the crew who were working on the Boat deck. They all worked admirably, but I think that if there had been better organisation the results would have been more satisfactory.

I heard much evidence as to the conduct of the boats after the *Titanic* sank and when there must have been many struggling people in the water, and I regret to say that in my opinion some, at all events, of the boats failed to attempt to save lives when they might have done so, and might have done so successfully. This was particularly the case of boat No. 1. (Hendrickson, 5011) (Symons, 11501, 11527) It may reasonably have been thought that the risk of making the attempt was too great; but it seems to me that if the attempt had been made by some of these boats it might have been the means of saving a few more lives. Subject to these few adverse comments, I have nothing but praise for both passengers and crew. All the witnesses speak well of their behaviour. It is to be remembered that the night was dark, the noise of the escaping steam was terrifying, the peril, though perhaps not generally recognised, was imminent and great, and many passengers who were unable to speak or to understand English, were being collected together and hurried into the boats.

Conduct of Sir Cosmo Duff Gordon and Mr Ismay

An attack was made in the course of the Enquiry on the moral conduct of two of the passengers, namely, Sir Cosmo Duff Gordon and Mr. Bruce Ismay. It is no part of the business of the Court to enquire into such matters, and I should pass them by in silence if I did not fear that my silence might been misunderstood. The very gross charge against Sir Cosmo Duff Gordon that, having got into No. 1 boat he bribed the men in it to row away from the drowning people is unfounded. (Duff Gordon, 12586 et seq.) I have said that the members of the crew in that boat might have made some attempt to save the people in the water, and that such an attempt would probably have been successful; but I do not believe that the men were deterred from making the attempt by any act of Sir Cosmo Duff Gordon's. At the same time I think that if he had encouraged to the men to return to the position where the *Titanic* had foundered they would probably have made an effort to do so and could have saved some lives.

As to the attack on Mr. Bruce Ismay, it resolved itself into the suggestion that, occupying the position of Managing Director of the Steamship Company, some moral duty was imposed upon him to wait on board until the vessel foundered. I do not agree. Mr. Ismay, after rendering assistance to many passengers, found "C" collapsible, the last boat on the starboard side, actually being lowered. No other people were there at the time. There was room for him and he jumped in. (Ismay, 18559) Had he not jumped in he would merely have added one more life, namely, his own, to the number of those lost.

Third Class Passengers

It had been suggested before the Enquiry that the third class passengers had been unfairly treated; that their access to the Boat deck had been impeded, and that when at last they reached that deck the first and second class passengers were given precedence in getting places in the boats. There appears to have been no truth in these suggestions. It is no doubt true that the proportion of third class passengers saved falls far short of the proportion of the first and second class, but this is accounted for by the greater reluctance of the third class passengers to leave the ship, by their unwillingness to part with their baggage, by the difficulty in getting them up from their quarters, which were at the extreme ends of the ship, and by other similar causes. The interests of the relatives of some of the third class passengers who had perished were in the hands of Mr. Harbinson, who attended the Enquiry on their behalf. He said at the end of his address to the Court:

> "I wish to say distinctly that no evidence has been given in the course of this case which would substantiate a charge that any attempt was made to keep back the third class passengers. I desire further to say that there is no evidence that when they did reach the Boat deck there was any discrimination practiced either by the officers or the sailors in putting them into the boats."

I am satisfied that the explanation of the excessive proportion of third class passengers lost is not to be found in the suggestion that the third class passengers were in any way unfairly treated. They were not unfairly treated.

Means taken to Procure Assistance

As soon as the dangerous condition of the ship was realized, messages were sent by the Master's orders to all steamers within reach. (Bride, 16508) At 12.15 a.m. the distress signal C.Q.D. was sent. This was heard by several steamships and by Cape Race. By 12.25, Mr. Boxhall, the fourth officer, had worked out the correct position of the *Titanic*, and then another message was sent: "Come at once, we have struck a berg." This was heard by the Cunard steamer *Carpathia*, which was at this time bound from New York to Liverpool and 58 miles away. The *Carpathia* answered, saying that she was coming to the assistance of the *Titanic*. This was reported to Captain Smith on the Boat deck. At 12.26 a message was sent out, "Sinking; cannot hear for noise of steam." Many other messages were also sent, but as they were only heard by steamers which were too far away to render help it is not necessary to refer to them. At 1.45 a message was heard by the *Carpathia*, "Engine room full up to boilers." The last message sent out was "C.Q.," which was faintly heard by the steamer *Virginian*. This message was sent at 2.17. It thus appears that the Marconi apparatus was at work until within a few minutes of the foundering of the *Titanic*.

Meanwhile Mr. Boxhall was sending up distress signals from the deck. (Boxhall, 15394) These signals (rockets) were sent off at intervals from a socket by No. 1 emergency boat on the Boat deck. They were the ordinary distress signals, exploding in the air and throwing off white stars. The firing of these signals began about the time that No. 7 boat was lowered (12.45 a.m.), and it continued until Mr. Boxhall left the ship at about 1.45. (15593, 15420)

Mr. Boxhall was also using a Morse light from the bridge in the direction of a ship whose lights he saw about half a point on the port bow of the *Titanic* at a distance, as he thought, of about five or six miles. (Lightoller, 14160) He got no answer. In all, Mr. Boxhall fired about eight rockets. There appears to be no doubt that the vessel whose lights he saw was the *Californian*. The evidence from the *Californian* speaks of eight rockets having been seen between 12.30

and 1.40. (Gill, 18156-61) (Stone, 7830 et seq.) The *Californian* heard none of the *Titanic*'s messages; she had only one Marconi operator on board and he was asleep.

Rescue by the SS *Carpathia*

On the 15th of April the S.S. *Carpathia*, 13,600 tons gross, of the Cunard Line, Mr. Arthur Henry Rostron, Master, was on her passage to Liverpool from New York. She carried some 740 passengers and 325 crew. (Rostron, 25361 et seq.)

On receipt of the *Titanic*'s first distress message the Captain immediately ordered the ship to be turned round and driven at her highest speed (17 1/2 knots) in the direction of the *Titanic*. (25385, 25390) He also informed the *Titanic* by wireless that he was coming to her assistance, and he subsequently received various messages from her. At about 2.40 a.m. he saw a green flare which, as the evidence shows, was sent up by Mr. Boxhall in No. 2 boat. From this time until 4 a.m. Captain Rostron was altering his course continually in order to avoid icebergs. (25401) He fired rockets in answer to the signals from Boxhall's boat. At 4 o'clock he considered he was practically up to the position given and he stopped his ship at 4.05. He sighted the first boat (No. 2) and picked her up at 4.10. There was then a large number of icebergs round him, and it was just daylight. Eventually, he picked up in all 13 lifeboats, two emergency boats and two collapsible boats, all of which were taken on board the *Carpathia*, the other boats being abandoned as damaged or useless. From these boats he took on board 712 persons, one of them died shortly afterwards. The boats were scattered over an area of four to five miles, and it was 8 a.m. before they had all been picked up. He saw very little wreckage when he got near to the scene of the disaster, only a few deck chairs, cork lifebelts, etc., and only one body. The position was then 41° 46′ N., 50° 14′ W.

The *Carpathia* subsequently returned to New York with the passengers and crew she had rescued.

The Court desires to record its great admiration of Captain Rostron's conduct. He did the very best that could be done.

Numbers Saved

The following were the numbers saved:

1st Class.

Adult males	57	out of	175	or 32.57	percent.
Adult females	140	out of	144	or 97.22	percent.
Male Children	5	All Saved			
Female Children	1	All Saved			
Total	203	out of	325	or 62.46	percent.

2nd Class.

Adult males	14	out of 168	or 8.33	percent.
Adult females	80	out of 93	or 86.02	percent.
Male Children	11			
Female Children	131			
Total	18	out of 285	or 41.40	percent.

3rd Class.

Adult males	75	out of 462	or 16.23	percent.
Adult females	76	out of 165	or 46.06	percent.
Male Children	13	out of 48	or 27.08	percent.
Female Children	14	out of 31	or 45.16	percent.
Total	178	out of 706	or 25.21	percent.

Total 499 out of 1,316, or 37.94 percent.

Crew Saved.

Deck Department	43 out of 66	or 65.15	percent.
Engine Room Department	72 out of 325	or 22.15	percent.
Victualling Department,	97 out of 494	or 19.63	percent.
(including 20 women out of 23)			

Total 212 out of 885, or 23.95 percent.
Total on board saved 711 out of 2,201, or 32.30 percent.

Passengers and Crew.

Adult males	338	out of 1,167	or 20.27	percent.
Adult females	316	out of 425	or 74.35	percent.
Children	57	out of 109	or 52.29	percent.

Total........... 711 out of 2,201, or 32.30 percent.

Circumstances in Connection with the SS *Californian*

It is here necessary to consider the circumstances relating to the S.S. *Californian*.

On the 14th of April, the S.S. *Californian* of the Leyland line, Mr. Stanley Lord, Master, was on her passage from London, which port she left on April 5th, to Boston, U.S., were she subsequently arrived on April 19th. She was a vessel of 6,223 tons gross and 4,038 net. Her full speed was 12 1/2 to 13 knots. She had a passenger certificate, but was not carrying any passengers at the time. She belonged to the International Mercantile Marine Company, the owners of the *Titanic*.

At 7.30 p.m., ship's time, on 14th April, a wireless message was sent from this ship to the *Antillian*. (Evans, 8941, 8943)

> "To Captain, '*Antillian*,' 6.30 p.m., apparent ship's time, lat. 42° 3' N., long. 49° 9' W. Three large bergs, 5 miles to southward of us. Regards. - Lord."

The message was intercepted by the *Titanic*, and when the Marconi operator (Evans) of the *Californian* offered this ice report to the Marconi operator of the *Titanic*, shortly after 7.30 p.m., the latter replied, "It is all right. I heard you sending it to the *Antillian*, and I have got it." (8972) (Lord, 6710)

The *Californian* proceeded on her course S. 89° W. true until 10.20 p.m. ship's time, when she was obliged to stop and reverse engines because she was running into field ice, which stretched as far as could then be seen to the northward and southward.

The Master told the Court that he made her position at that time to be 42° 5' N., 57° 7' W. (6704) This position is recorded in the log book, which was written up from the scrap log book by the Chief Officer. The scrap log is destroyed. It is a position about 19 miles N. by E. of the position of the *Titanic* when she foundered, and is said to have been fixed by dead reckoning and verified by observations. I am satisfied that this position is not accurate. The Master "twisted her head" to E.N.E. by the compass and she remained approximately stationary until 5.15 a.m. on the following morning. The ship was slowly swinging round to starboard during the night. (6713) (Groves, 8249)

At about 11 p.m. a steamer's light was seen approaching from the eastward. The Master went to Evans' room and asked, "What ships he had." The latter replied: "I think the *Titanic* is near us. I have got her." (Evans, 8962, 8988) The Master said: "You had better advise the *Titanic* we are stopped and surrounded by ice." This Evans did, calling up the *Titanic* and sending: "We are stopped and surrounded by ice." (8993) The *Titanic* replied: "Keep out." The *Titanic* was in communication with Cape Race, which station was then sending messages to her. (8994) The reason why the *Titanic* answered, "Keep out," (9004) was that her Marconi operator could not hear what Cape Race was saying, as from her proximity, the message from the *Californian* was much stronger than any message being taken in by the *Titanic* from Cape Race, which was much further off. (9022) Evans heard the *Titanic* continuing to communicate with Cape Race up to the time he turned in at 11.30 p.m.

The Master of the *Californian* states that when observing the approaching steamer as she got nearer, he saw more lights, a few deck lights, and also her green side light. He considered that at 11 o'clock she was approximately six or seven miles away, and at some time between 11 and 11.30, he first saw her green light, she was then about 5 miles off. (Lord, 6761) He noticed then about 11.30 she stopped. In his opinion this steamer was of about the same size as the *Californian*; a medium-sized steamer, "something like ourselves." (6752)

From the evidence of Mr. Groves, third officer of the *Californian*, who was the officer of the first watch, it would appear that the Master was not actually on the bridge when the steamer was sighted.

Mr. Groves made out two masthead lights; the steamer was changing her bearing slowly as she got closer, (Groves, 8147) and as she approached he went to the chart room and reported this to the Master; he added, "she is evidently a passenger steamer." (8174) In fact, Mr. Groves never appears to have had any doubt on this subject: In answer to a question during his examination, "Had she much light?" he said, "Yes, a lot of light. There was absolutely no doubt of her being a passenger steamer, at least in my mind." (8178)

Gill, the assistant donkeyman of the *Californian*, who was on deck at midnight said, referring to this steamer: "It could not have been anything but a passenger boat, she was too large." (Gill, 18136)

By the evidence Mr. Groves, the Master, in reply to his report, said: "Call her up on the Morse lamp, and see if you can get any answer." This he proceeded to do. The Master came up and joined him on the bridge and remarked: "That does not look like a passenger steamer." (Groves, 8197) Mr. Groves replied "It is, sir. When she stopped, her lights seemed to go out, and I suppose they have been put out for the night." (8203) Mr. Groves states that these lights went out at 11.40, and remembers that time because "one bell was struck to call the middle watch." (8217) The Master did not join him on the bridge until shortly afterwards, and consequently after the steamer had stopped.

In his examination Mr. Groves admitted that if this steamer's head was turning to port after she stopped, it might account for the diminution of lights, by many of them being shut out. Her steaming lights were still visible and also her port side light. (8228)

The Captain only remained upon the bridge for a few minutes. (8241) In his evidence he stated that Mr. Groves had made no observations to him about the steamer's deck lights going out. (Lord, 6866) Mr. Groves' Morse signalling appears to have been ineffectual (although at one moment he thought he was being answered), and he gave it up. He remained on the bridge until relieved by Mr. Stone, the second officer, just after midnight. In turning the *Californian* over to him, he pointed out the steamer and said: "she has been stopped since 11.40; she is a passenger steamer. At about the moment she stopped she put her lights out." (Stone, 7810) When Mr. Groves was in the witness-box the following questions were put to him by me:

> "Speaking as an experienced seaman and knowing what you do know now, do you think that steamer that you know was throwing up rockets, and that you say was a passenger steamer, was the *Titanic*? - Do I think it? -Yes. - From what I have heard subsequently? -Yes. - Most decidedly I do, but I do not put myself as being an experienced man. -But that is your opinion as far as your experience goes? - Yes, it is, my Lord."

(Groves, 8441)

Mr. Stone states that the Master, who was also up (but apparently not on the bridge), pointed out the steamer to him with instructions to tell him if her bearings altered or if she got any closer; he also stated that Mr. Groves had called her up on the Morse lamp and had received no reply. (Stone, 7815)

Mr. Stone had with him during the middle watch an apprentice named Gibson, whose attention was first drawn to the steamer's lights at about 12.20 a.m. (Gibson, 7424) He could see a masthead light, her red light (with glasses) and a "glare of white lights on her after deck." He first thought her masthead light was flickering and next thought it was a Morse light, "calling us up." (7443) He replied, but could not get into communication, and finally came to the conclusion that it was, as he had first supposed, the masthead light flickering. Some time after 12.30 a.m., Gill, the donkeyman, states that he saw two rockets fired from the ship which he had been observing, (Gill, 18156-61) and about 1.10 a.m., Mr. Stone reported to the Captain by voice pipe, they he had seen five white rockets from the direction of the steamer. (Stone, 7870) He states that the Master answered, "Are they Company's signals?" and that he replied, "I do not know, but they appear to me to be white rockets." The Master told him to "go on Morsing," and, when he received any information, to send the apprentice down to him with it. (7879) Gibson states that Mr. Stone informed him that he had reported to the Master, and that the Master had said the steamer was to be called up by Morse light. (Gibson, 7479) This witness thinks the time was 12.55; he at once proceeded again to call the steamer up by Morse. He got no reply, but the vessel fired three more white rockets; these rockets were also seen by Mr. Stone.

Both Mr. Stone and the apprentice kept the steamer under observation, looking at her from time to time with their glasses. Between 1 o'clock and 1.40 some conversation passed between them. Mr. Stone remarked to Gibson: "Look at her now, she looks very queer out of water, her lights look queer." (7515) He also is said by Gibson to have remarked, "A ship is not going to fire rockets at sea for nothing;" (7529) and admits himself that he may possibly have used that expression. (Stone, 7894)

Mr. Stone states that he saw the last of the rockets fired at about 1.40, and after watching the steamer for some twenty minutes more he sent Gibson down to the Master.

> "I told Gibson to go down to the Master, and be sure to wake him, and tell him that altogether we had seen eight of these white lights like white rockets in the direction of this other steamer; that this steamer was disappearing in the

southwest, that we had called her up repeatedly on the Morse lamp and received no information whatsoever."

Gibson states that he went down to the chart room and told the Master; that the Master asked him if all the rockets were white, and also asked him the time. (Gibson, 7553) Gibson stated that at this time the Master was awake. It was five minutes past two, and Gibson returned to the bridge to Mr. Stone and reported. They both continued to keep the ship under observation until she disappeared. Mr. Stone describes this as "A gradual disappearing of all her lights, which would be perfectly natural with a ship steaming away from us."

At about 2.40 a.m. Mr. Stone again called up the Master by voice pipe and told him that the ship from which he had seen the rockets come had disappeared bearing SW. 1/2 W., (Stone, 7976) the last he had seen of the light; and the Master again asked him if he was certain there was no colour in the lights. "I again assured him they were all white, just white rockets." (7999) There is considerable discrepancy between the evidence of Mr. Stone and that of the Master. The latter states that he went to the voice pipe at about 1.15, but was told then of a white rocket (not five white rockets). (Lord, 6790) Moreover, between 1.30 and 4.30, when he was called by the chief officer (Mr. Stewart), he had no recollection of anything being reported to him at all, although he remembered Gibson opening and closing the chart room door. (6859)

Mr. Stewart relieved Mr. Stone at 4 a.m. (Stewart, 8571) The latter told him he had seen a ship four or five miles off when he went on deck at 12 o'clock, and 1 o'clock he had seen some white rockets, and that the moment the ship started firing them she started to steam away. (8582) Just at this time (about 4 a.m.) a steamer came into sight with two white masthead lights and a few lights amidships. He asked Mr. Stone whether he thought this was the steamer which had fired rockets, and Mr. Stone said he did not think it was. At 4.30 he called the Master and informed him that Mr. Stone had told him he had seen rockets in the middle watch. (8615) The Master said, "Yes, I know, he has been telling me." (8619) The Master came at once on to the bridge, and apparently took the fresh steamer for the one which had fired rockets, (8632) and said, "She looks all right; she is not making any signals now." This mistake was not corrected. He, however, had the wireless operator called.

At about 6 a.m. Captain Lord heard from the *Virginian* that the "*Titanic* had struck a berg, passengers in boats, ship sinking"; and he at once started through the field ice at full speed for the position given. (Lord, 7002)

Captain Lord stated that about 7.30 a.m. he passed the *Mount Temple*, (7014) stopped, and that she was in the vicinity of the position given him as where the *Titanic* had collided (lat. 41° 46′ N.; long. 50° 14′ W.). (7026) He saw no wreckage there, but did later on near the *Carpathia*, which ship he closed soon afterwards, and he stated that the position where he subsequently left this wreckage was 41° 33′ N.; 50° 1′ W. It is said in the evidence of Mr. Stewart that the position of the *Californian* was verified by stellar observations at 7.30 p.m. on the Sunday evening, and that he verified the Captain's position given when the ship stopped (42° 5′ N.; 50° 7′ W.) as accurate on the next day. The position in which the wreckage was said to have been seen on the Monday morning was verified by sights taken on that morning.

All the officers are stated to have taken sights, and Mr. Stewart in his evidence remarks that they all agreed. (Stewart, 8820) If it is admitted that these positions were correct, then it follows that the *Titanic*'s position as given by that ship when making the C.Q.D. signal was approximately S. 16° W. (true), 19 miles from the *Californian*; and further that the position in which the *Californian* was stopped during the night, was thirty miles away from where the wreckage was seen by her in the morning, or that the wreckage had drifted 11 miles in a little more than five hours.

There are contradictions and inconsistencies in the story as told by the different witnesses. But the truth of the matter is plain. (7020) The *Titanic* collided with the berg 11.40. The vessel seen by the *Californian* stopped at this time. The rockets sent up from the *Titanic* were distress signals. The *Californian* saw distress signals. The number sent up by the *Titanic* was about eight. The *Californian* saw eight. The time over which the rockets from the *Titanic* were sent up was from about 12.45 to 1.45 o'clock. It was about this time that the *Californian* saw the rockets. At 2.40 Mr. Stone called to the Master that the ship from which he'd seen the rockets had disappeared.

At 2.20 a.m. the *Titanic* had foundered. It was suggested that the rockets seen by the *Californian* were from some other ship, not the *Titanic*. But no other ship to fit this theory has ever been heard of.

These circumstances convince me that the ship seen by the *Californian* was the *Titanic*, and if so, according to Captain Lord, the two vessels were about five miles apart at the time of the disaster. The evidence from the *Titanic* corroborates this estimate, but I am advised that the distance was probably greater, though not more than eight to ten miles. The ice by which the *Californian* was surrounded was loose ice extending for a distance of not more than two or three miles in the direction of the *Titanic*. The night was clear and the sea was smooth. When she first saw the rockets the *Californian* could have pushed through the ice to the open water without any serious risk and so have come to the assistance of the *Titanic*. Had she done so she might have saved many if not all of the lives that were lost.

Board of Trade's Administration

The Court was invited by the Board of Trade "to report upon the Rules and Regulations made under the Merchant Shipping Acts 1894-1906, and the administration of those Acts, and of such Rules and Regulations so far as the consideration thereof is material to this casualty" (No. 26 of the questions submitted to the Court by the Board of Trade). (B. T. Deptl, Pap. 246.) Charges were made against the Board of Trade during the progress of the Enquiry of a twofold kind. First, it was said that the Board had been negligent in that they had failed to keep up to date their Rules and Regulations relating generally to the provision of life-saving appliances at sea, and secondly it was said that their officials had in the particular instance of the *Titanic* failed to exercise due care in the supervision of the vessel's plans and the inspection of the work done upon her.

With reference to the first of these charges, it was reduced in the course of the Enquiry to a charge of neglect to keep the Board's scale for the provision of lifeboat accommodation up to date. The circumstances are these. In March, 1886, the Board appointed a Departmental Committee consisting of three of their principal officers to inquire into the question of boats, rafts and life-saving apparatus carried by seagoing merchant ships. (Howell, 22268) In their report this Committee pointed out that as regards boats for ocean-going steamers carrying large numbers of passengers, the boats would be of little use in saving life (although they might for a time prolong its existence) unless succour were at hand from other ships or from proximity to shore; and speaking with special reference to passenger steam vessels carrying emigrants across the Atlantic to ports on the east coast of North America, they said as follows:

> "Considering the number of vessels employed in this Trade, and the large number of passengers they carry, and also taking into consideration the stormy character of the ocean they have to cross, and the thick and foggy weather encountered, we think this class is the most important of any, and we cannot pass over the fact that of late years this traffic has been carried on with remarkable immunity from loss of life.
>
> The boat accommodation these vessels are forced to carry when sailing with emigrants is regulated by the scale in the Passengers Act, 1855, which provides for boat accommodation for 216 people as a maximum, so that supposing a vessel leaves with 1,000 passengers and 200 crew under the present statutory requirements, she need only carry sufficient boat accommodation for 216 of these people. Thus it will be seen that the boats carried by this class of vessel are also quite inadequate as an effectual means of saving life should a disaster happen to a ship with her full complement of passengers on board. We are glad to be able to say that there are many liberal and careful shipowners who do all in their power to provide for the safety of their passengers by equipping their vessels with boats far in excess of the number required by statute. But, at the same time, there are others carrying large numbers of emigrants who do no more than they are required to do by law.
>
> We have gone into this question with reference to this class of vessel very fully, and have visited many of them, and we think that the boats required by the Act should be increased 100 per cent, and in addition to them that the owners should be induced to carry sufficient collapsible boats and approved rafts, so that each ship shall have sufficient life-saving gear for all on board at any one time, provided, as said before, that no ship need carry more boat accommodation than is sufficient for all on board at that time."

In 1887 a Select Committee of the House of Commons, of which Lord Charles Beresford was the Chairman, was appointed to report on Saving Life at Sea, and they found in the report "That many passengers ships could not, without great inconvenience, carry so many of the ordinary wooden boats as would suffice to carry the whole of the passengers and crew with safety in bad weather. (22272-5) Under such circumstances the crew would not be sufficient to man so many boats; nor could they all be got into the water in sufficient time in the event of very rapid foundering. Having regard, however, to the fact that accidents occur probably as often in moderate weather as in bad, and having regard also to the fact that the very cause the accident frequently incapacitates many of the boats, and to the further fact that insufficiency of boats undoubtedly tends to cause panic, we are the opinion that all sea-going passenger ships should be compelled by law to carry such boats, and other life-saving apparatus, as would in the aggregate best provide for the safety of all on board in moderate weather."

As a result of these reports, the "Merchant Shipping (Life Saving Appliances) Act, 1888," appears to have been passed, under which rules were made by the Board of Trade at different dates. The Merchant Shipping Act, 1894, repealed the Act of 1888, and substituted therefore sections 427 to 431 and the seventeenth schedule of the new Act. Under this Act (1894), a table showing the minimum number of boats to be placed under davits, and their minimum cubic contents was issued by the Board. It was dated the March 9, 1894, and came into operation on 1 June of that year. This table was based on the gross tonnage of the vessels to which it was to apply, and not upon the numbers carried, and it provided that the number of boats and their capacity should increase as the tonnage increased. The table, however, stopped short at the point were the gross tonnage of the vessels reached "10,000 and upwards." As to all such vessels, whatever their size might be, the minimum number of boats under davits was fixed by the table at 16, with a total minimum capacity of 5,500 cubic feet.

But as regarded emigrant steamships there was a rule which provided that if the boats under davits required by the table did not furnish sufficient accommodation for all on board, then additional boats of approved description (whether under davits or not) or approved life rafts should be carried, and that these additional boats or rafts should be of at least such carrying capacity that they and the boats required by the table should provide together in vessels of 5,000 tons and upwards three-fourths more than the minimum cubic contents required by the table, so that in the case of an emigrant ship such as the *Titanic* the requirements under the rules and table together exacted a provision of 9,625 cubic feet of lifeboat and raft accommodation (5,500 feet in boats under davits with three-fourths, namely, 4,125, added). Taken at 10 cubic feet per person, this would be equivalent to a provision for 962 persons. No doubt at the time these rules were made and this table was drawn up it was thought that, having regard to the size of vessels then built and building, it was unnecessary to carry the table further. The largest emigrant steamer then afloat was the *Lucania*, of 12,952 tons.

In the report of the Select Committee of the House of Commons a reference to watertight bulkheads had been made, which was in the following terms:

> "Though the question of construction was clearly not included in the reference to the Committee, still they think it only right to state, after having heard the evidence, that the proper placing of bulkheads, so as to enable a ship to keep afloat for some length of time after an accident has occurred, is most important for saving life at sea, and a thing upon which the full efficiency of life-saving appliances largely depends."

This passage probably explains the insertion in the Board of Trade's Rules for Life Saving Appliances of Rule No. 12, which is as follows:

> "Watertight compartments. - When ships of any class are divided into efficient watertight compartments to the satisfaction of the Board of Trade, they shall only be required to carry additional boats, rafts and buoyant apparatus of one-half of the capacity required by these Rules, but the exemption shall not extend to life-jackets or similar approved articles of equal buoyancy suitable to be worn on the person."

If this rule had become applicable to the *Titanic*, then the total cubical lifeboat or raft accommodation which she would have been required to carry would have not have been more than 7,562 (equivalent to accommodation for 756 persons). It did not, however, become applicable for the owners never required the Board of Trade to express any opinion under the rule as to the efficiency of the watertight compartments. The *Titanic*, in fact, carried boat accommodation for 1,178 persons, a number far in excess of the requirements of the Table and Rules, and, therefore, no concession under Rule 12 was needed. Speaking generally, recourse to this Rule 12 by shipowners has been so insignificant that the Rule itself may be regarded as of no practical account.

The foregoing Rules with the Table were laid before Parliament in the usual way, and so received the required statutory sanction.

After 1894 steamers were built of a much larger tonnage than 10,000, the increase culminating in the *Titanic*, with a gross tonnage of 46,328. As the vessels built increased in size, so one would have thought the necessity for increased lifeboat accommodation would grow; but the Rules and Table remained stationary, and nothing was done to them by way of change. The explanation of this long delay (from 1894-1912) was given before me by Sir Alfred Chalmers, who had served under the Board of Trade as Nautical Advisor from 1896 to August, 1911. (Chalmers, 22875) He is now retired. I think it will be well if I give his explanation in his own words. He says:

> "I considered the matter very closely from time to time. I first of all considered the record of the trade - that is to say, the record of the casualties - and to see what immunity from loss there was. I found it was the safest mode of travel in the world, and I thought it was neither right nor the duty of a State Department to impose regulations upon that mode of travel as long as the record was a clean one. Secondly, I found that, as ships grew bigger, there were such improvements made in their construction that they were stronger and better ships, both from the point of view of watertight compartments and also absolute strength, and I considered that that was the road along which the shipowners were going to travel, and that they should not be interfered with. I then went to the maximum that is down in the Table - 16 boats and upward, together with the supplementary boats, and I considered from my experience that that was the maximum number that could be rapidly dealt with at sea and that could be safely housed without encumbering the vessel's decks unduly. In the next place, I considered that the traffic was very safe on account of the routes - the definite routes being agreed upon by the different companies, which tended to lessen the risk of

collision, and to avoid ice and fog. Then, again, there was the question of wireless telegraphy, which had already come into force on board of these passenger ships. I was seized of the fact that in July, 1901, the *Lucania* had been fitted with wireless telegraphy, and the Cunard Line, generally, fitted it during that year to all their ships. The Allan line fitted it in 1902, and I am not sure that in 1904 it had not become quite general on the trans-Atlantic ships. That, of course, entered into my consideration as well. Then another point was the manning. It was quite evident to me that if you went on crowding the ships with boats you would require a crew which were not required otherwise for the safe navigation of the ship, or for the proper upkeep of the ship, but you are providing a crew which would be carried uselessly across the ocean, that never would be required to man the boats. Then the last point, and not the least, was this, that the voluntary action of the owners was carrying them beyond the requirements of our scale, and when voluntary action on the part of shipowners is doing that, I think that any State Department should hold its hand before it steps in to make a hard-and-fast scale for that particular type of shipping. I considered that that scale fitted all sizes of ships that were then afloat, and I did not consider it necessary to increase it, and that was my advice to Sir Walter Howell."

I appreciate this explanation, and I think there is much force in it. At the same time, it seems to me that it does not justify the delay. Even taking all these matters into consideration, it cannot be that the provision for boat accommodation made in 1894 for vessels of 10,000 tons and upwards remained sufficient to 1910, when vessels of 45,000 tons were being built. Two considerations demonstrate this. The first is that some shipowners recognised the insufficiency of the requirements of the Board of Trade, and voluntarily exceeded those requirements by providing larger boat accommodation than the old Rules and Table exacted. The second is that shortly before Sir Alfred Chalmers left the Board of Trade, the Board had begun to direct attention to the amending of their Rules in this connection.

It appears that in November, 1910, a question was asked in the House of Commons as to whether the attention of the President of the Board of Trade had been called to the fact that the *Olympic*, a sister ship of the *Titanic*, was provided with 14 lifeboats only. (22755) The answer given was that the *Olympic* (which was then in course of construction) would carry 14 lifeboats and two ordinary boats of an aggregate capacity of 9,752 cubic feet, which was in excess of the requirements of the Statutory Rules. On the 15th February, 1911, a further question was asked as to the date of the last Regulations, and whether, having regard to the increased tonnage of modern ships, the desirability of revising the Regulations would be considered by the Board of Trade. The answer by the President was:

> "Those Regulations were last revised in 1894. The question of their further revision is engaging the serious attention of the Board of Trade, and I have decided to refer the matter to the Merchant Shipping Advisory Committee for consideration and advice."

Three days afterwards, namely, on the 18th of February, 1911, a circular letter was sent out by the Board of Trade to the Board's principal officers at Liverpool, London and Glasgow, asking each of those gentlemen to draft such an extension of the existing boat scale as he might think satisfactory and reasonable for the conditions of large passenger steamers. The circular letter was answer by the principal officer in Glasgow (Mr. Harris) on the 24th February, 1911, by the principal officer in London (Mr. Park) on the 27th February, 1911, and by the principal officer in Liverpool (Mr. Young) on the 3rd March, 1911. It is sufficient to say of these answers that they all suggested a large extension of the statutory requirements.

Meanwhile, namely, on the 28th February, 1911, Mr. Archer, the Board of Trade's principal ship surveyor, had also drawn up a scale. (Archer, 24246) This was a more exacting scale than that of any of the three principal officers. By his scale a vessel of the tonnage of the *Titanic* would have had to carry boat accommodation equivalent to at least 24,937 cubic feet, which would have been sufficient to hold all, and more than all, the persons who were on board at the time of the disaster (2,201). It would not, however, have been nearly sufficient to have held all that the vessel might lawfully have carried, viz., 3,547, and it is to be observed with reference to Mr. Archer's scale that in it he suggests an extension of Rule 12, by which (if the vessel were divided into efficient watertight compartments) the total boat accommodation might be reduced much more than Rule 12 as it stands would permit. If this reduction be taken into account, the boat accommodation would fall so that it would be sufficient for only 1,750 persons. Mr. Archer's view was that shipowners should be encouraged to increase flotability of the ships they built, and that the way to encourage them was to relax the legal requirements as to boats as their plans advanced in that direction. The great object was so to build the ship that in the event of the disaster she would be her own lifeboat.

(It may be mentioned that Mr. Archer stated in the witness-box that since the disaster to the *Titanic* he had modified his views and thought that Rule 12 should be discontinued. (Archer, 24256))

Having obtained these four reports, the Board of Trade, on the 4th April, 1911, submitted the matter to their Advisory Committee, and obtained the Committee's report on the 4th July, 1911. The following are copies (with omissions of immaterial passages) of the Board of Trade's letter of the 4th April, 1911, and of the Advisory Committee's report of the 4th July, 1911:

> Board of Trade, Marine Department,
>
> 7, Whitehall Gardens, London, S. W.,
>
> April 4, 1911.
>
> SIR,
>
> I am directed by the Board of Trade to enclose herewith, for the information of the Merchant Shipping Advisory Committee, a copy of a question asked in the House of Commons on the 15th February and of the answer given by the President of the Board of Trade with reference to the Life-Saving Appliances Rules made under section 427 of Merchant Shipping Act, 1894.
>
> The Board are of opinion that the Table in the Appendix to the Rules should be extended upwards in the form indicated in the accompanying scale, so as to provide for vessels of tonnage up to 50,000 tons gross and upwards.
>
> It appears to the Board that the number of boats and the boat capacity need not necessarily increase in a regular proportion according to the increase in tonnage, and that due regard should be paid to what is reasonable and practicable in passenger steamers exceeding 10,000 tons.
>
> I am to state that the Board would be obliged if the Merchant Shipping Advisory Committee would be so good as to suggest in what manner the scale (see accompanying copy)

should be continued upwards having due regard to the considerations indicated above.

I am further to state that the Board would be glad to learn whether the Advisory Committee are of opinion that Rule 12 should or should not be revised so as to exempt altogether from the requirement of additional boats and/or rafts those vessels which are divided into efficient watertight compartments to the satisfaction of the Board of Trade.

I am, etc,

(Signed) Walter J. Howell.

The Secretary,

Merchant Shipping Advisory Committee.

MERCHANT SHIPPING ADVISORY COMMITTEE.

4th July, 1911.

SIR,

We have the honour to report that your letter of the 4th April with reference to the minimum number of lifeboats to be carried on vessels of 10,000 tons gross tonnage and upwards, and your letter of the 17th May on the subject of the depth of lifeboats, have been very carefully considered by the Merchant Shipping Advisory Committee, and that it was unanimously decided at a meeting held on the 29th ultimo to adopt the report of a Sub-Committee which was specially appointed to inquire into these questions.

A copy of the report is accordingly forwarded herewith, and the Committee desire us to suggest for the consideration of the Board of Trade, that effect should be given to the recommendations contained in it.

We are, etc.,

(Signed) NORMAN HILL, Chairman.

(Signed) R. W. MATTHEW, Secretary.

Report of Life-Saving Appliances Subcommittee

Sir Walter J. Howell,
Assistant Secretary,
Marine Department,
Board of Trade.

In accordance with the decision of the Merchant Shipping Advisory Committee at their meeting on Friday, the 28th April, we have given careful consideration to the letter of the 4th April from the Board of Trade, in which the Committee were asked to advise:

1. as to the manner in which the Table in the Appendix to the Life-Saving Appliances Rules should be extended so as to provide for vessels of tonnage up to 50,000 tons gross and upwards; and

2. as to whether Rule 12 should, or should not, be revised so as to exempt altogether from the requirement of additional boats and/or rafts, those vessels which are divided into efficient watertight compartments to the satisfaction of the Board of Trade.

In considering these questions, we have had specially in mind the fact that the number of passengers carried does not necessarily increase in proportion to the increase in the tonnage of the vessel. This is particularly true in the case of vessels exceeding 10,000 tons, a type of vessel which is practically only built to provide special accommodation for large numbers of first and second class passengers.

Similarly there is no fixed relation between the tonnage of vessels and the deck space available for the carrying of lifeboats under davits. Increase in the length of a vessel is only one of the factors, and often not the most material factor contributing to the increase in its tonnage, and it should also be remembered, in estimating the space available for the launching of lifeboats, that it is impossible to place davits forward of the bridge, and very undesirable to have them on the quarters of the vessel.

We are strongly of opinion that every encouragement should be given to secure the provision of vessels which by their construction have been rendered as unsinkable as possible, and which are provided with efficient means for communicating with the shore or other vessels in the case of disaster.

In view of these considerations, we have agreed upon the following recommendations:

1. That it is questionable whether it is practicable to increase the number of davits;

2. That any increase in the number of lifeboats to be carried can probably be best effected by providing for the launching of further boats from the existing davits;

3. That the Table should be extended in the manner indicated below, viz.:

Gross Tonnage.	Minimum Number of Boats to be placed under davits.	Min. No. of Additional boats to be readily available for attachment to Davits.	Total Min. Cub. Contents of boats req. by Col. 2 and 3.
10,000 and under 12,000	16	-	5,500
12,000 and under 20,000	16	2	6,200
20,000 and under 35,000	16	4	6,900
35,000 and under 45,000	16	6	7,600
45,000 and upwards	16	8	8,300

It is further recommended that all passenger vessels of 10,000 tons gross tonnage and upwards should be required to be fitted with wireless telegraphy apparatus;

4. That the Rules should be amended so as to admit of decked lifeboats of an approved type being stowed on top of one another or under an open lifeboat, subject to suitable arrangements being made for launching promptly the boats so stowed;

5. That the additional boats and rafts required under the provisions of Division A, class 1 (d) of the Life-Saving Appliances Rules shall be of at least such carrying capacity that they, and the boats required by columns 2 and 3 of the above Table, provide together three-fourths more than the minimum cubic contents required by column 4 of that Table;

6. That vessels divided into efficient watertight compartments to the satisfaction of the Board of Trade should (provided they are fitted with wireless telegraphy apparatus) be exempt from the requirement

of additional boats and/or rafts. The Committee suggest, in this connection, that the Board of Trade should review the requirements designed to attain the standards as to watertight compartments at present enforced by them under Rule 12, having regard to the developments of shipbuilding since the report of the Committee on the spacing and construction of watertight bulkheads.

We have also had before us the Board's further letter of the 17th May enquiring whether, in the opinion of the Advisory Committee, it would be advisable to prescribe a maximum depth for lifeboats as compared with their breadth, and, if so, what that proportion should be.

In connection with this letter, we have been supplied by the Board of Trade with reports from their principal officers in Great Britain, giving the dimensions and cubic capacities of the various kinds of boats of five typical ships in each of eight ports.

We recommend that the Board should be advised to alter the Life-Saving Appliances Rules so as to provide that, in future, the depth of lifeboats supplied to a British Merchant vessel shall not exceed 44 percent of their breadth.

(Signed)
NORMAN HILL,
A. M. CARLISLE,
S. CROSS,
WM. THEODORE DOXSFORD,
GEO. N. HAMPSON,
ROBERT A. OGILVIE,
T. ROYDEN,
T. ROME,
THOMAS SPENCER,
J. HAVELOCK WILSON.

It will be observed that if effect had been given by the Board of Trade to the Report of the Advisory Committee the requirements for a vessel of the size of the *Titanic* would have reached 14,525 cubic feet (8,300 plus ¾ths of 8,300, namely, 6,225), with, however, this qualification that if the vessel were divided into efficient watertight compartments (as she probably was) and fitted with wireless telegraphy (as she certainly was) a provision of boat capacity of 8,300 cubic feet, equivalent to space for 830 persons, would have been legally sufficient. This would have been much less than the accommodation with which the *Titanic* when she put to sea was, in fact, provided (namely 1,178 persons).

Effect, however, was not given to the report. A question arose with reference to the dimensions of lifeboats, and it was thought better to get that question settled before proceeding to revise the rules. The examination of this question involved making several experiments which caused delay; and it was not until the 16th April, 1912, that a reply was sent by the Board of Trade to the Advisory Committee. It will be noticed that the date of this reply is just after the disaster to the *Titanic* became known. I am, however, quite satisfied that instructions for the preparation of this letter had been given in the offices of the Board of Trade some days before the 16th, and that the letter was not sent in consequence of the disaster. It is desirable to set it out.

> Board of Trade, Marine Department,
>
> 7, Whitehall Gardens, London, S. W.,
>
> 16th April, 1912.
>
> SIR,
>
> With reference to your letter of the 4th July last respecting certain question raised in connection with the proposed revision of the Life-Saving Appliances Rules, I am directed by the Board of Trade to state, for the information of the Advisory Committee, that they have given very careful consideration to the report of the Life-Saving Appliances Sub-Committee which was forwarded with your letter.
>
> As regards the recommendations with reference to the proposed extension of the Table (Appendix to the Life-

Saving Appliances Rules) showing the minimum number of boats to be placed under davits, the Board are glad to observe that the Committee agree that alterations and additions are now necessary to meet the changed conditions due to recent developments in the size of passenger steamships and in the number of persons which these vessels can accommodate. The Board of Trade note that the gradations of tonnage in the extension of the scale suggested by the Advisory Committee are not the same as those in the form of scale submitted to them by the Board; while the increase in the number of boats is not in the number to be placed under davits, but in the number of additional boats required to be readily available for attachment to davits. It is observed that the Committee hold the view that "it is questionable whether it is practicable to increase the number of davits," and "that any increase in the number of lifeboats to be carried can "probably be best effected by providing for the launching of further boats from the existing davits."

The Board presume that, in arriving at these conclusions, the Committee have had regard to ships already built rather than to new ships, as they see no reason why there would be any difficulty in having more than eight pairs of davits on each side of the ship, provided that the requirements of Life-Saving Appliances Rules were known before the plans were prepared. The Board are of opinion that a very careful and thorough revision of the Table should now be made, and I am to transmit herewith a copy of a memorandum and tables prepared by the Professional Advisor to the Marine Department, containing a full and considered opinion on the subject of the extension of the boat scale and cognate questions.

As regards the proposed amendment of the Rules, so as to admit of decked lifeboats of an approved type being stowed one above another, or under an open lifeboat, I am to state that this question is now under consideration, and a communication will be addressed to you shortly on the subject.

With reference to the Advisory Committee's recommendation regarding the amendment of Rule 12 of the General Rules, the Board desire me to state that the questions raised in the recommendation are of wide application, and of such importance that the Board do not think that they can be adequately considered except by Committee of equal standing to the Committee which reported in 1891 on the Spacing and Construction of Watertight Bulkheads in the Mercantile Marine. The Board have the question of the appointment of a Committee under consideration.

In connection with the Advisory Committee's recommendation that the depth of lifeboats shall not exceed 44 percent of their breadth, I am to transmit herewith, for their consideration, a draft amendment of Rules Nos. 1, 2, and 3 of the General Rules with reference to the construction of ships' boats.

The Board have made full enquiry into the question of the construction of ships' boats, and obtained some useful information as to the average depth of boat which is deemed desirable for safety and utility, and the ratio of that depth to the breath, and they attach so much importance to this element of boat construction that they think it should receive the careful attention of the Committee. The Board think that the Committee, in light of this additional information, may reconsider the opinions expressed on this point in their letter of the 4th July.

I am therefore to transmit herewith copies of memoranda by the Professional Advisor to the Marine Department and acting Principal Ship Surveyor.

The Board desire me to state that they would be glad to be furnished with the Advisory Committee's views as to the application of the proposed new rules and boat scale, e.g., whether they should apply to ships already built, and, if so, to what extent. They regard it as of great importance, on the one hand, that all British vessels should be provided with a proper and sufficient equipment of life-saving appliances, and, on the other, that regulations should not be enforced without notice which would necessitate important structural alterations and consequent heavy expense in vessels already built.

I am to add that in order to make the constitution of the Committee, when considering this question, agree with that of the Statutory Life-Saving Appliances Committee indicated in the Seventeenth Schedule to the Merchant Shipping Act, 1894, the Board have followed the course adopted on previous occasions, and have invited Lloyd's Register of British and Foreign Shipping and the Institute of London Underwriters to select a representative who will be available to sit on the Advisory Committee when the question is under consideration.

I am, etc.,

(Signed) Walter J. Howell.

The Secretary,

Merchant Shipping Advisory Committee,

7, Whitehall Gardens, S. W.

Extension of Life-Saving Apparatus Tables

It will be seen that I have given priority in importance to the form of ships' boats rather than to their number on the principle that a few reliable boats are of greater value than a large number of indifferent ones; but if the former desirable condition can be obtained by the proposed alterations in our Rules as to measurement, &c., we are freer to approach the question of adding to the number of boats provided for in the existing tables.

As with the question of ratio D: B dealt with by the Advisory Committee last year, so with the question of boat increase and relative increase of cubic capacity dealt with by them on the same occasion, perhaps the Board might inform the Committee that they are not satisfied that a slightly different recommendation might not have been made had the matter been still further considered at the time.

Referring to the table of boat capacities computed by them particularly it might be helpful if the Board laid before them for consideration the table, which I attach hereto and submit, as showing a more reasonable proportionate increase in capacity than appears so far, in my opinion, in the other papers before us. It will be seen in this statement that the number of boats recommended by the Advisory

Committee is practically retained, but the unit of increase in capacity is put at 300 cubic feet.

Perhaps I should state here what actuated me in fixing upon this rate of increase. I realised that in all probability it would become the practice on these large liners to provide boats under davits which would contain the entire cubic feet required by the L. S. A. Rules, that is - the quantity required by rule under davits plus the addition of 3/4ths and it occurred to me that if, after the figure 5,500 cubic feet the increase of capacity were uniform and moderate it would result in a total at 1 3/4 which would by incidence fit in with the scale of boats already recommended as requisite in the report of the Advisory Committee and in my own, i.e., assuming that the boats are of 500 cubic feet. Example: take a vessel of 30,000 tons and under 35,000 tons, according to the table I submit she would be required to have by the 1 3/4 rule a total boat capacity of 12,250 cubic feet which at 500 cubic feet per boat equals 24 boats nearly. There should be no difficulty on the large ships in carrying this quantity under davits, i.e., 18 directly under davits and six boats inboard.

Please see incidental table attached.

A. H. Y.

8.13.12

(Mr. A. H. Young, Professional Advisor to the Board of Trade.)

Proposed Extension of Boat Scale

Gross Tons	Boats.	Minimum Total Cub. Cnts. of boats required to be carried under Davits.
10,000 and under 12,000	16	5,500 c. ft.
12,000 and under 15,000	18	5,800 c. ft.
15, 000 and under 20,000	20	6,100 c. ft.
20,000 and under 25,000	22	6,400 c. ft.
25,000 and under 30,000	24	6,700 c. ft.
30,000 and under 35,000	24	7,000 c. ft.
35,000 and under 40,000	24	7,300 c. ft.
40,000 and under 45,000	24	7,600 c. ft.
45,000 and under 50,000	26	7,900 c. ft.
50,000 and upwards.	26	8,200 c. ft.

Please see the accompanying incidental table showing how this number of boats can provide for the three-quarters additional capacity also, if only about 500 cubic feet per boat to 600 cubic feet.

A. H. Y.

Table of incidence (informative).

Gross Tons.	Number of Boats.	Cubic Feet.	C. ft. Additional	Tot. C. ft. at 1 ¾	Equivalent Boats
10,000 and under 12,000	16	5,500	4,125	9,625	19 say or 16
12,000 and under 15,000	18	5,800	4,350	10,150	20 " " 16
15,000 and under 20,000	20	6,100	4,575	10,675	21 " " 18
20,000 and under 25,000	22	6,400	4,800	11,200	22 " " 19
25,000 and under 30,000	24	6,700	5,025	11,725	24 " " 20
30,000 and under 35,000	24	7,000	5,250	12,250	24 " " 20
35,000 and under 40,000	24	7,300	5,475	12,775	25 " " 21
40,000 and under 45,000	24	7,600	5,700	13,300	26 " " 22
45,000 and under 50,000	26	7,900	5,925	13,825	27 " " 23
50,000 and upwards.	26	8,200	6,150	14,350	28 " " 24

One-fourth of the above boats may be carried inboard, but they should not exceed 500 cubic feet in capacity, so that they may be readily drawn up to the davits.A. H. Y.30.312.

Draft Amendment of General Rules

(1) Boats. - All boats shall be constructed and properly equipped as provided by these rules, and shall be of such form and proportions that they shall have sufficient freeboard, and ample stability in a seaway, when loaded with their full complement of persons and equipment.

All thwart and side seats must be fitted as low in the boat as practicable, and bottom boards must be fitted so that the thwarts shall not be more than 2 ft. 9 in. above them.

All boats and other life-saving appliances are to be kept ready for use to the satisfaction of the Board of Trade. Internal buoyancy apparatus may be constructed of wood, or of copper or yellow metal of not less than 18 oz. to the superficial foot, or of other durable material.

Section (A). A boat of this section shall be a lifeboat of the whaleboat form, properly constructed of wood or metal, having for every 10 cubic ft. of her capacity, computed as in Rule (2), at least 1 cubic ft. of strong and serviceable inclosed air-tight compartments, so constructed that water cannot find its way into them. In the case of metal boats an addition will have to be made to the cubic capacity of air-tight compartments, so as to give them buoyancy equal to that of the wooden boat.

Section (B). A boat of this section shall be a lifeboat, of whaleboat form, properly constructed of wood or metal, having inside and outside buoyancy apparatus together equal in efficiency to the buoyancy apparatus provided for a boat of section (A). At least one-half of the buoyancy apparatus must be attached to the outside of the boat.

Section (C). A boat of this section shall be a lifeboat, properly constructed of wood or metal, having some buoyancy apparatus attached to the inside and/or outside of the boat, equal in efficiency to one-half of the buoyancy apparatus provided for a boat of section (A) or section (B).

At least one-half of the buoyancy apparatus must be attached to the outside the boat.

Section (D). A boat of this section shall be a properly constructed boat of wood or metal.

Section (E). A boat of this section shall be a boat of approved construction, form, and material, and may be collapsible.

(2) Cubic Capacity. - The cubic capacity of an open boat, and of a deck boat of section (D) or section (E) shall be ascertained by multiplying the product of the length, breadth, and depth by 6, subject, however, to the following provisions:-

The length shall be measured from the foreside of the rabbet on the stem to the afterside of the rabbet on the stern post, and the breadth shall be measured from the outside of plank to the outside of plank amidships. The actual depth shall be measured from the top of the gunwale to the top of the bottom plank next to the keel, but the depth used in calculating the cubic capacity shall not in any case exceed 3.6 ft., and if the actual depth is equal to or less than 3.6 ft., the depth used in calculating the cubic capacity shall not exceed 45 percent of the breadth measured as indicated above.

If the oars are pulled in rowlocks, the bottom of the rowlock is to be considered as the gunwale in measuring the depth of the boat.

If any question is raised requiring absolute accuracy, the cubic capacity of a boat shall be ascertained by Stirling's rule; subject to the foregoing provisions as to depth.

(3) Number of Persons for Boats.

(A) - Subject to the provisions of paragraph's (b), (c) and (d) of this clause the number of persons an open boat of section (A) shall be deemed fit to carry shall be the number of cubic feet ascertained as in Rule (2) divided by 10, and the number of persons an open boat of section (B) or section (C), or an open or decked boat of section (D) or section (E) shall be deemed fit to carry shall be the number of cubic feet ascertained as in Rule (2) divided by 8. The space in the boat shall be sufficient for the seating of the persons carried in it, and for the proper use of the oars.

(B) - An open boat of section (A) or section (B) or section (C) or section (D) or section (E), shall not be deemed to be fit to carry the number of persons ascertained as in paragraph (a) of this clause unless the boat is so constructed that it has a mean shear of at least half an inch for each foot of its length, and that the boat's half-girth amidships measured outside the planking from the side of the keel to the top of the gunwale is at least equal to nine-tenths of the sum of the boat's depth inside and half its maximum breadth amidships, and that the mean of the half-girths measured in the same manner at two points, one-quarter of the length of the boat from the stem and stern-post respectively, is at least equal to eight-tenths of the sum of the depth inside and half the maximum breadth amidships.

(C.) - A decked boat of section (D) or section (E) shall not be deemed to be fit to carry the number of persons ascertained as in paragraph (a) of this clause, unless the top of the deck amidships is at a height above the water approved by the Board of Trade, when the boat is so loaded.

(D) - If the surveyor is doubtful as to the number of persons any open or decked boat is fit to carry, he may require the boat to be tested afloat with the intended number of persons on board.

(E) - The rules numbers 1, 2, and 3, as now amended, are not to be retrospective, and are to apply only to boats built after.

Ship's Boats

The salient feature of the Reports of the Board's officers on the subject is the consensus of opinion that the form of a boat is the chief factor to be considered in determining its value as a life-saving appliance.

It has been found that while there are many boats of good form supplied to ships, there is yet a large proportion where the boats are not only not so good, but which can only be regarded as unsafe if they had on board anything approaching the number of persons for which they measure.

It is the latter type we are chiefly concerned with; how is it that the form has so deteriorated as to create this concern in our minds? I think the cause is not far to seek; it appears to be the outcome of (1) The shipowner's desire to carry the maximum number of persons in the minimum number of boats; (2) in the efforts of the shipbuilder, as a rule, to carry out the specification in which he has contracted supply the owners with boats at a price, often very low, and naturally he does not sublet his contract with the boatbuilder at a loss; (3) the aim of the competing boatbuilder, which is to build his boats at as little cost price as possible, and yet to provide accommodation for the prescribed number of persons. He is probably limited as to length, and therefore relies on the breadth and depth, in this direction, he is unintentionally assisted by the Board's rule for measurement, viz., (L x B X D x6)/10 or 8; so long, therefore, as he can obtain his breadth at one point for measurement purposes, it is quite immaterial to him how soon he fines away to the ends, with a result that the stability of the boat becomes almost entirely dependent upon the form of a very limited midship section, or the still smaller proportion of same that would be under water when in the loaded condition.

The boat builder may be further restricted as to breadth, and, therefore, he again detracts from the form a boat should have by dispensing with shear and increasing the depth from keel to gunwale amidships. This method of building boats enables him to obtain the capacity required by the owner at the expense of the boat's stability and utility.

No doubt when the Life-Saving Appliances Rules came into being, the divisors 10 and 8 for the different sections were deemed safe on the supposition that the usual full form of boat would not be largely departed from; experience has shown, however, that form is frequently sacrificed for the unworthy objects referred to above, and it follows, therefore, that either the form should be improved or a heavier divisor laid down.

It would, I think, be more effective to deal with form, and devise a rule by which we can insure that a boat will be reasonably safe with its load, not merely in smooth water - as in our recent test - but in a sea-way. It is essential, therefore, to draw the attention of the Advisory Committee to the value the Board attach to form, and particularly to that part of it underwater, emphasising the great necessity there is for an increase to the bearing surface of the underwater portion of boats, and this end can, no doubt, be best attained by the putting into practice of the suggestions made by the Principal Ship Surveyor for amending the rules, and which aim at prolonging the form or fullness of dimension of the midship body underwater well towards the ends of the boat. It is well known that by extending the body in this way greater buoyancy and stability are secured without materially affecting the speed. It is often supposed that defective stability due to bad form can be rectified by the disposition of the persons or things, but anyone with real experience of boats in a sea-way cannot fail to realise that this is the wrong principle to work on; granted, therefore, that the question of form must take priority - how can it be best attained? And if we refer to Mr. Archer's method of measurement, as stated in his amendment to the Rules, it will be seen how simple and effective it is. For the purpose of illustration we might take the model of a ship's boat obtained through the Board's surveyors at Glasgow, the dimensions of which enlarged to scale represent a boat of (L) 30.0 X (B) 8.5 X (D) 3.5 and is an embodiment of the proportions amidships and at quarter distance from each end, proposed by Mr. Archer.

It cannot be too strongly urged that for a ship's lifeboat to be fit to carry the number of persons it measures for in any degree of safety, whenever it may be required at sea, the underwater or bearing surface should be carried out to the ends as much as possible and all straight lines avoided. The bows of many of the existing types of boat are examples of the worst possible form for safety, and the counters are as bad - if they can be said to have any.

Depth. - It appears from the reports that the most generally approved ratio of depth to the breadth is 4/10. This has been established, not only by our long experience, but by the numerous tests recently conducted by the Board's surveyors at various ports, and the attention of the Advisory Committee might be drawn to this fact.

It is, of course, necessary also to have a good freeboard, but a well-proportioned boat does not require so much freeboard as the commoner type, as with proper sheer and underwater surface she is easy in a sea-way. If the gunwale is too high there is loss of power over the oars, which is serious when for the safety of the boat she is required to be kept head-on to sea, and with a fresh breeze, even in a good boat, this is not always an easy matter.

It is a matter for consideration that at the tests made by our surveyors the conditions were most favorable, being usually in smooth water of a sheltered dock, and, in not a few instances, considerable anxiety was felt for the safety of those on board when crowded in accordance to the existing rules. If it was thus in smooth water one dare hardly contemplate the results in a sea-way. If the shipowner does not see to it that a safe type of boat is provided, then the number of persons to be accommodated in boats which do not come up to proportions deemed safe by the Board of Trade should be very considerably curtailed.

A. H. Y.,
23.3.12.

Construction of Ship's Boats

It will, I think, be useful to consider the principle factors that govern the dimensions of boats forming part of the life-saving apparatus in merchant ships.

The minimum number and capacity of boats are determined by the regulations, and the capacity is determined by the product of the length, breadth, and depth of the boats. As the space on the ship in which to stow the boats is generally limited, it is generally found easier to increase their depth than the length or breadth, and this is further encouraged, I believe, by the cost of boats being quoted at so much per foot in length. The builder or owner determines the dimensions of the boat; the boatbuilder is concerned merely with the construction and, in most cases, usually their form or lines.

Attention has been called by the Mark Lane Surveyors to the form and proportions of the boats used in the Royal Navy. The proportion of depth to breadth is greater than is apparent from the particulars given, as all boats larger than a 30-ft. gig have 6 1/2 in. washboards above the gunwale, and even the gigs and many of the smaller boats have portable washboards. It must also be remembered that all the Navy boats are square-sterned, except the whaleboat, and are designed with easy lines so as to make good sailers, no air cases are fitted, and the seats are kept very low. The boats are not provided simply as life-saving appliances; as a matter of fact the life-saving equipment of a warship is extremely small.

It is true that each type of boat is given a certain "life-saving capacity," which is ascertained by crowding in as many men as practicable with the boat in still water and all equipment on board. This number agrees closely with that obtained by the Board's rule (L x B x D x6) /8. These boats, moreover, have a much smaller freeboard than is considered desirable in the merchant navy; but the occupants are all under discipline and in charge of experienced seaman. In the Mercantile Marine it may, and often does, happen, that the boats are crowded with panic-stricken men, women, and children, and instances have occurred, I believe, wherein there has not been a single man in the boat who has ever handled an oar before. Having these points in view, I do not agree that the navy type of boat is the most suitable for our purpose.

The chief desiderata in a ship's boat as a life-saving appliance are:

(1) To carry the maximum number of people without overcrowding; and with

(2) A reasonable amount of stability and freeboard;

(3) And without undue interference with the use of oars.

(1) Is almost wholly dependent on the length and breadth of the boat; provided (2) is satisfied; depth has very little influence on it. For

example, take a boat 30 × 9 × 3.5, 567 cubic ft. by our rule, as a section (D) or (E) boat it should carry 567/8 = 72 people; such a boat should allow (30 × 9 × 8)/ 72 = 3 sq. ft. of area per person at the gunwale, which should be ample if all sit in the bottom who cannot find seating room on the side benches or thwarts.

(2) Stability and freeboard are dependent upon the boat's breadth, depth, and form. The element of length does not enter into it, and it would be most unreasonable to limit the ratio of length to breadth, as suggested from Liverpool, or to limit the depth to the cube root of the length, as proposed by one of the London surveyors. Mr. Gemmell gives particulars, M. 26,298, of four boats tested, which proved to have ample accommodation and stability for the complements allowed by the regulations; the ratio of depth to breadth varied from 0.41 to 0.45.

Captain O'Sullivan also reported five boats which he tested with ratios of D to B, varying from 0.4 to 0.44, all except one being satisfactory, the exception being rather tender and overcrowded, due to poor lines. The freeboards of all these boats when loaded were, I think, sufficient. The depth in no case exceeded 3.6, and only in one case did the ratio exceed 0.44.

The Surveyors, Liverpool, tested a boat 3.75 deep and having a ratio of $D/b = 0.41$, which proved satisfactory.

Captain Griffiths tested a boat 4.1 deep, having a ratio $D/b = 0.455$, which he considered to be unsafe with the full complement on board.

The consensus of opinion is that the depth should not exceed 3 ft. 5 in. or 3 ft. 6 in., and the ratio of D/b should not exceed 0.44. This, however, is not sufficient to guarantee sufficient seating and stability. Captain Clarke tested a boat 24.4 × 6.55 × 2.45, which was very unsafe with the rule complement on board. The ratio D/b is only 0.38 in this case. It will be seen, however, that this craft has exceptionally fine lines and is evidently quite unsuited to carry the rule complement. It is quite evident that the form of the boat must be taken into account.

The dimensions of boats vary so greatly that generally the boatbuilder builds his boats "to the eye," using only a midship mould; it follows that the forms of boats of the same dimensions will vary considerably and with different workmen. Something more is required than a limitation in the ratio of depth to breadth. It is desirable that the sheer should be ample, and the form not unduly fined away within the midship half length. From consideration of the particulars and lines of the boats mentioned in the surveyor's reports, I think a simple rule to regulate the form may be devised such as I will indicate later.

It is, I think, necessary to limit the depth as a factor for ascertaining the number to be accommodated. The increase of depth beyond a certain point, while unduly increasing the number of people that may be carried, increases proportionately the required air case capacity, to meet which the seats have to be raised with a corresponding increase in the height of the centre of gravity and decrease in the stability and difficulty in rowing. A boat 3.6 deep would have the thwarts about 3 ft. above the bottom, and any increase in this height makes it difficult for an ordinary man to row when sitting down. In rough sea the men would have very little control over the oars if standing up. A further objection to the very deep boat is its small stability in the light condition. It is not, I believe, an unusual occurrence for such boats to capsize in rough weather, before the passengers or crew can be got into them, and I have myself seen such a boat capsize in dock with only two men in it; due to lumpy water and a stiff breeze catching it on the beam when coming out of the shelter afforded by the dock wall.

I do not think, however, any limit of depth should be imposed, except as a measure of capacity. Any rules that may be devised should be such as are of easy and ready application, and which will not bear harshly on the boats that have already been accepted. I therefore suggest that the present rules will sufficiently meet the case, with the following modification.

In no case should the depth to be used in General Rule (2) exceed 3.6 ft. and 45 percent of the breadth. In all cases where the actual depth is 45 percent of the breadth or less, the maximum number of persons, as ascertained by Rule (3) should not be allowed unless the boat has been found capable of carrying that number by actual test in the water, or unless the boat has at least 1/2 in. of sheer per foot of length, and the half-girth amidships, measured outside the plank, from the side of the keel to the top of the gunwale, is at least 90 percent of the sum of the depth and the half breadth, and the mean of the half girths as similarly measured at one quarter the boat's length from the stem and stern post are least 80 percent of the sum of the midship depth and half breadth.

The thwarts and side benches should be kept as low as practicable, and the bottom boards should be so fitted that the height of the thwarts above them will not exceed 2 ft. 9 in.

A. J. D.

27.1.12

It should be stated that the new Committee on Bulkheads mentioned in the paragraph of this letter which deals with Rule 12 has now been formed.

Subsequently Sir Walter Howell wrote and sent three letters to the Advisory Committee which were as follows:

> Board of Trade, Marine Department,
>
> 7, Whitehall Gardens, London, S. W.,
>
> 20th April, 1912.
>
> Immediate.
>
> SIR,
>
> With reference to previous correspondence between the Department and your Committee respecting the revision of the statutory rules for Life-Saving Appliances on British ships, and particularly to the letter from this Department of the 16th April, I am directed by the Board of Trade to state that as an entirely new situation has been created by the recent disaster to the S.S. *Titanic* they assume that the Committee, in reconsidering the matter in connection with the suggestions already put before them by the Board will have full regard to this new situation, and the facts of the disaster so far as ascertained.
>
> As you are doubtless aware, suggestions have been made in the House of Commons and elsewhere to the effect that, in view of the loss of the *Titanic*, action should be taken by the Board of Trade in regard to certain questions other than those expressly dealt with in the Life-Saving Appliances

Rules, e.g., in regard to (1) steamship routes in the North Atlantic; (2) the speed of steamers where there may be dangers to navigation; and (3) the provision and use of searchlights on large passenger steamers; and the Board would be glad to know the Committee's views in regard to these, and any other suggestions which may have come to their knowledge, intended to diminish the risk, or to mitigate the effects of accidents to passenger vessels at sea.

I am, &c.

The Secretary,

Merchant Shipping Advisory Committee.

(Signed) WALTER J. HOWELL.

Board of Trade, Marine Department,

7, Whitehall Gardens, London, S. W.,

24th April, 1912.

SIR,

With reference to previous correspondence between this Department and your Committee respecting the revision of the statutory rules for Life-Saving Appliances on British ships, and particularly to the letter from this Department of the 16th April, in which you were informed that the question of the proposed amendment of the rules so as to admit of decked lifeboats being stowed one above another or one under an open lifeboat, was under consideration. I am directed by the Board of Trade to state, for the information of your Committee, that the Board of Trade will be glad if the Committee will consider whether any, and if so, what, amendment of the rules, and in particular of the Rule of the 19th April, 1910, and of the Rule of the 14th June, 1911, are in their opinion desirable with the object of supplementing the boats immediately under davits by as much additional boat accommodation as is practicable, having regard to the new situation which has been created by the recent disaster to the S.S. *"Titanic."* A plan illustrating the principle is being prepared so as to be in readiness for your Committee by Friday.

I am, &c.,

The Secretary,

Merchant Shipping Advisory Committee.

(Signed) WALTER J. HOWELL.

Board of Trade, Marine Department,

7, Whitehall Gardens, London, S. W.,

25th April, 1912.

SIR,

With reference to previous correspondence respecting the proposed revision of the statutory regulations as to boats and life-saving appliances on ships, I am directed by the Board of Trade to state, for the information of the Merchant Shipping Advisory Committee, that, apart from the questions which have been raised regarding the boat accommodation on vessels over 10,000 tons, it seems desirable to consider whether the provision of boats and other life-saving appliances required by the rules in the case of vessels under 10,000 tons is satisfactory, or whether the rules or the boat scale should be altered in respect of their application to such vessels; and the Board would be glad to be favoured with the observations of the Committee on this point in addition to those that have already been referred to them.

I am, &c.,

The Secretary,

Merchant Shipping Advisory Committee.

(Signed) WALTER J. HOWELL.

To these letters the Advisory Committee sent the following answer:

Merchant Shipping Advisory Committee,

7, Whitehall Gardens, London, S. W.,

27th April, 1912.

SIR,

We are desired by the Merchant Shipping Advisory Committee to inform you that your letters of the 16th, 20th, 24th, and 25th instant were brought before the Committee at a meeting held yesterday.

The Committee fully recognize that the proved impossibility of keeping such a vessel as the *Titanic* afloat after a collision with ice, until the arrival of outside succour, has created an entirely new situation which was neither in the contemplation of the Board of Trade nor of the Committee in the consideration of the extension of the existing boat scale in regard to vessels of 10,000 tons and upwards.

In advising on such extension in July last, the Committee aimed at providing ample boat accommodation on large passenger vessels in accordance with principles that were adopted by the original Life-Saving Appliances Committee, and which principles had apparently been fully justified by many years of experience. It is with satisfaction that the Committee note that the Board of Trade, apart from the new possibilities demonstrated by the loss of the "*Titanic*," agreed in the essentials with the recommendation of the Committee. In face of the new facts, the Committee at their meeting yesterday re-opened entirely the question of the revision of the boat scale for large passenger vessels with a view of providing the maximum of protection for the passengers and crew in the event of an overwhelming disaster, whilst, at the same time, maintaining the principles in regard to the stability and sea-going qualities of the ship itself, and to the prompt and efficient handling of the boats carried under the existing scale, which hitherto have proved not only essential to safety, but also adequate for all ordinary emergencies. The questions involved are not free from difficulty, but they will receive the immediate attention of the Committee. Pending their consideration, the Committee note that assurances have been received by the Board of Trade from representatives of most of the large passenger lines to the effect that every effort will be made to equip their vessels, at the earliest possible moment, with boats and rafts sufficient to accommodate all persons on board.

In regard to the recommendation forwarded with the Committee's letter of the 4th July last, that the Board of Trade should, having regard to the developments in shipbuilding since the Report of the Committee of 1894 on Spacing and Construction of Watertight Bulkheads, review the requirements designed to attain the standards at present enforced under Rule 12, the Advisory Committee note that the Board of Trade have under consideration the appointment of a Committee of equal standing to that of the Committee of 1894. In view of the great importance of this question the Advisory Committee desire us respectfully to urge that such a Committee be appointed at as early a date as possible.

The subject of the general revision of the statutory regulations as to boats and life-saving appliances on all ships, which, apart from the questions regarding the boat accommodation on vessels over 10,000 tons, is for the first time referred to the Advisory Committee by the letter of the 25th instant, together with the particular questions raised in the letters of the 16th, 20th, and 24th instant, are also receiving the immediate attention of the Committee.

At yesterday's meeting sub-committees were appointed to give immediate consideration to the subjects requiring detailed examination. These sub-committees will pursue their enquiries concurrently, and we are desired by the Advisory Committee to inform you that their investigation into the revision of the Life-Saving Appliances Rules will be proceeded with as expeditiously as possible.

We are, &c.,

Sir Walter J. Howell, K. C. B., Assistant Secretary,

Marine Department, Board of Trade.

(Signed) NORMAN HILL, Chairman.

(Signed) R. W. MATTHEW, Secretary.

This letter was acknowledged by the Board of Trade on the 10th May, 1912, as follows:

Board of Trade, Marine Department,

7, Whitehall Gardens, London, S. W.,

10th May, 1912.

SIR,

I am directed by the Board of Trade to acknowledge the receipt of, and to thank you for, your letter of the 27th April, stating that their letters of the 16th, 20th, 24th, and 25th April, have been considered by the Merchant Shipping Advisory Committee.

The Board observe with satisfaction that, in view of the entirely new situation which has arisen, the Advisory Committee have decided to re-open the question of the revision of the Table in the Life-Saving Appliances Rules in so far as it governs the boat accommodation in vessels over 10,000 tons gross. The Board are further glad to observe that the question of a general revision of the Life-Saving Appliances Rules is also under consideration by the Committee, and in this connection they presume that, in considering the question of a general revision of the rules including the Table, the Committee will consider the principles on which the requirements as to boat accommodation should be based, including, inter alia, whether the Table should continue to be based on tonnage. Any conclusion reached by the Committee on this question would naturally affect the revision of the present Table as applying to vessels of more than 10,000 tons, upon which the Committee has already been engaged.

The Board agree with the view expressed by the Advisory Committee that the appointment of another Committee on the Spacing and Construction of Watertight Bulkheads is desirable. Steps have already been taken by the President to form such a Committee, and he hopes to be able to announce the names within a few days. A further communication on this point will be addressed to the Committee in the course of a few days.

The Board are glad to note that Sub-Committees have been appointed to deal concurrently with the subjects requiring detailed consideration in connection with the revision of the Life-Saving Appliances Rules.

The Board desire me to add that they assume that the Committee, in considering the matters referred to them, will have regard to all important aspects of the question of Life-Saving Appliances, whether expressly dealt with in the Statutory Rules or not, and in particular to the essential question of the adequacy of the provision for lowering and manning the boats and rafts carried by vessels.

I am, etc.,

The SECRETARY,

Merchant Shipping Advisory Committee.

7, Whitehall Gardens, London, S. W.

(Signed) WALTER J. HOWELL.

This finishes the history of the action of the Board of Trade in relation to the provision of boat accommodation on emigrant ships. The outstanding circumstance in it is the omission, during so many years, to revise the rules of 1894, and this, I think, was blameable, notwithstanding the excuse or explanation put forward by Sir Alfred Chalmers. I am, however, doubtful whether even if the Rules had been revised, the change would have been such as to have required boat accommodation which would have increased the number of lives saved. Having regard to the recommendations of the Advisory Committee, the Board of Trade would probably not have felt justified in making Rules which would have required more boat accommodation than that with which the *Titanic* was actually provided; and it is not to be forgotten that the *Titanic* boat accommodation was utilised to less than two-thirds of its capacity. These considerations, however, afford no excuse for the delay of the Board of Trade.

The gross tonnage of a vessel is not, in my opinion, a satisfactory basis on which to calculate the provision of boat accommodation. Hitherto, I believe, it has been accepted as the best basis by all nations. But there seems much more to be said in favour of making the number of lives carried the basis and for providing boat or raft accommodation for all on board. Rule 12 of the Life-Saving Appliances Rules of 1902, which deals with watertight compartments and boat accommodation, ought to be abolished. The provision of such compartments is of supreme importance but it is clear that it should not be sought at the expense of a decrease in boat accommodation. When naval architects have devised practical means for rendering ships unsinkable, the question of boat accommodation may have to be reconsidered, but until that time arrives boat accommodation should, where practicable, be carried for all on board. This suggestion may be thought by some to be extravagant. It has never been enforced in the mercantile marine of Great Britain, nor, as far as I know, in that of any foreign nation. But it appears, nevertheless, to be admitted by all that is possible without undue inconvenience or undue interference with commerce to increase, considerably in many cases, the accommodation hitherto carried, and it seems, therefore, reasonable that the law should require an increase to be made. As far as foreign going passenger and emigrant steamships are concerned, I am of opinion that, unless justification be shown for deviating from this course, such ships should carry boats or rafts for all on board.

With reference to the second branch of the complaint against the Board of Trade, namely that their officials had failed to exercise due care in the supervision of the vessel's plans and in the inspection of the work done upon her, the charges broke down. Suggestions were made that the Board's requirements fell short of those of Lloyd's Registry; but no evidence was forthcoming to support the suggestions. The investigation of the charges took much time, but it only served to show that the officials had discharged their duties carefully and well.

Powers of the Board Re Design of Vessels

The *Titanic* was efficiently designed and constructed to meet the contingencies which she was intended to meet.

The bulkheads were of ample strength. They were sufficiently closely spaced and were carried up in the vessel to a height greater than sufficient to meet the requirements of 1894 Bulkheads Committee.

But I am advised that the ship could have been further subdivided so that she would probably have remained afloat longer than she did. The Board of Trade have, however, apparently no power to exercise any real supervision in the matter of subdivision. All they have express power to insist upon in this connection with respect to any steam vessel is that there shall be four watertight bulkheads - a provision quite inadequate for safety in a collision damaging the vessel about the collision bulkhead. They can also, if invited by the shipowner (but not otherwise), exercise supervision under Rule 12. This supervision, I am told, they have been invited to exercise in only 103 cases over a period of 18 years. In 69 of these cases the Board have expressed their satisfaction with the subdivision provided. It seems to me that the Board should be empowered to require the production of the designs of all passenger steamers at an early period of their construction and to direct such alterations as may appear to them to be necessary and practicable for the purpose of securing proper watertight subdivision.

Findings of the Court

It is now convenient to answer the twenty-six questions submitted by the Board of Trade.

S. S. *TITANIC*.

1. When the *Titanic* left Queenstown on or about 11th April last:

(a.) What was the total number of persons employed in any capacity on board her, and what were their respective ratings?

(b.) What was the total number of her passengers, distinguishing sexes and classes, and discriminating between adults and children?

Answer:

(a) The total number of persons employed in any capacity on board the *Titanic* was: 885

The respective ratings of these persons were as follows:

Deck Department	66
Engine	325
Compartment	494
Victualling Department	885

N.B. - The eight bandsmen are not included in this number as their names appear in the second-class passenger list.

(b.) The total number of passengers was 1,316. Of these:

	Male	Female	Total
1st Class	180	145	325
2nd Class	179	106	285
3rd Class	510	196	706
			1,316

Of the above, 6 children were in the first-class, 24 in the second-class, and 79 in the third-class. Total 109.

2. Before leaving Queenstown on or about 11th April last did the *Titanic* comply with the requirements of the Merchant Shipping Acts, 1894-1906, and the rules and regulations made thereunder with regard to the safety and otherwise of "passenger steamers" and "emigrant ships"?

Answer:

Yes.

3. In the actual design and construction of the *Titanic* what special provisions were made for the safety of the vessel and the lives of those on board in the event of collisions and other casualties?

Answer:

These have been already described.

4. (a.) Was the *Titanic* sufficiently and efficiently officered and manned? (b.) Were the watches of the officers and crew usual and proper? (c.) Was the *Titanic* supplied with proper charts?

Answer:

(a.) Yes.

(b.) Yes.

(c.) Yes.

5. (a.) What was the number of the boats of any kind on board the *Titanic*? (b.) Were the arrangements for manning and launching the boats on board the *Titanic* in case of emergency proper and sufficient? (c.) Had a boat drill been held on board, and, if so, when? (d.) What was the carrying capacity of the respective boats?

Answer:

(a.) 2 Emergency boats.

... 14 lifeboats.... 4 Englehardt boats.

(b.) No, but see discussion.

(c.) No.

(d.) The carrying capacity of the:

.... 2 Emergency boats was for 80 persons.

... 14 Lifeboats was for 910 persons.

... 4 Englehardt boats was for 188 persons.

... or a total of 1,178

6. (a.) What installations for receiving and transmitting messages by wireless telegraphy were on board the *Titanic*? (b.) How many operators were employed on working such installations? (c.) Were the installations in good and effective working order, and were the number of operators sufficient to enable messages to be received and transmitted continuously by day and night?

Answer:

(a.) A Marconi 5 Kilowatt motor generator with two complete sets of apparatus supplied from the ship's dynamos, with an independent storage battery and coil for emergency, was fitted in a house on the Boat Deck.

(b.) Two.

(c.) Yes.

7. (a.) At or prior to the sailing of the *Titanic* what, if any, instructions as to navigation were given to the Master or known by him to apply to her voyage? (b.) Were such instructions, if any, safe, proper and adequate, having regard to the time of year and dangers likely to be encountered during the voyage?

Answer:

(a.) No special instructions were given, but he had general instructions contained in the book of Rules and Regulations supplied by the Company. (see "Sailing Orders.")

(b.) Yes, but having regard to subsequent events they would have been better if a reference hadto be adopted in the event of reaching the region of ice.

8. (a.) What was in fact the track taken by the *Titanic* in crossing the Atlantic Ocean? (b.) Did she keep to the track usually followed by liners on voyages from the United Kingdom to New York in the month of April? (c.) Are such tracks safe tracks at that time of year? (d.) Had the Master any, and, if so, what discretion as regards the track to be taken?

Answer:

(a.) The Outward Southern Track from Queenstown to New York, usually followed in April by large steam vessels. (see)"Route Followed.")

(b.) Yes, with the exception that instead of altering her course on approaching the position 42° N., 47° W. she stood on her previous course for some 10 miles further South West, turning to S. 86° W. true at 5.50 p.m.

(c.) The Outward and Homeward bound Southern tracks were decided on as the outcome of many years' experience of the normal movement of ice. They were reasonably safe tracks for the time of year, provided, of course, that great caution and vigilance when crossing the ice region were observed.

(d.) Yes. Captain Smith was not fettered by any orders and to remain on the track should information as to position of ice make it in his opinion undesirable to adhere to it. The fact, however, of Lane Routes having been laid down for the common safety of all, would necessarily influence him to keep on (or very near) the accepted route, unless circumstances as indicated above should induce him to deviate largely from it.

9. (a.) After leaving Queenstown on or about the 11th April last, did information reach the *Titanic* by wireless messages or otherwise by signals of the existence of ice in certain latitudes? (b.) If so, what were such messages or signals and when were they received, and in what position or positions was the ice reported to be, and was the ice reported in or near the track actually being followed by the *Titanic*? (c.) Was her course altered in consequence of receiving such information, and, if so, in what way? (d.) What replies to such messages or signals did the *Titanic* send, and at what times?

Answer:

(a.) Yes.

(b.) See particulars of ice messages already set out (see) "Ice Messages Received.")

(c.) No. Her course was altered as hereinbefore described, but not in consequence of the information received as to ice.

(d.) The material answers were:

At 12.55 p.m. S.S. *Titanic*. "To Commander, *Baltic*. Thanks for your message and good wishes. Had fine weather since leaving. Smith."

At 1.26 p.m. S.S. *Titanic*. "To Captain, *Caronia*. Thanks for message and information. Have had variable weather throughout. Smith."

10. (a.) If at the times referred to in the last preceding question or later the *Titanic* was warned of or had reason to suppose she would encounter ice, at what time might she have reasonably expected to encounter it? (b.) Was a good and proper look-out for ice kept on board? (c.) Were any, and, if so, what directions given to vary the speed - if so, were they carried out?

Answer:

(a.) At, or even before, 9.30 p.m. ship's time, on the night of the disaster.

(b.) No. The men in the crow's-nest were warned at 9.30 p.m. to keep a sharp look-out for ice; the officer of the watch was then aware that he had reached the reported ice region, and so also was the officer who relieved him at 10 p.m. Without implying that those actually on duty were not keeping a good look-out, in view of the night being moonless, there being no wind and perhaps very little swell, and especially in view of the high speed at which the vessel was running, it is not considered that the look-out was sufficient. An extra look-out should, under the circumstances, have been placed at the stemhead, and a sharp look-out should have been kept from both sides of the bridge by an officer.

(c.) No directions were given to reduce speed.

11. (a.) Were binoculars provided for and used by the look-out men? (b.) Is the use of them necessary or usual in such circumstances? (c.) Had the *Titanic* the means of throwing searchlights around her? (d.) If so, did she make use of them to discover ice? (e.) Should searchlights have been provided and used?

Answer:

(a.) No.

(b.) No.

(c.) No.

(d.) No.

(e.) No, but searchlights may at times be of service. The evidence before the Court does not allow of a more precise answer.

12. (a.) What other precautions were taken by the *Titanic* in anticipation of meeting ice? (b.) Were they such as are usually adopted by vessels being navigated in waters where ice may be expected to be encountered?

Answer:

(a.) Special orders were given to the men in the crow's-nest to keep a sharp look-out for ice, particularly small ice and growlers. The fore scuttle hatch was closed to keep everything dark before the bridge.

(b.) Yes, though there is evidence to show that some Masters would have placed a look-out at the stemhead of the ship.

13. (a.) Was ice seen and reported by anybody on board the *Titanic* before the casualty occurred? (b.) If so, what measures were taken by the officer on watch to avoid it? (c.) Were they proper measures and were they promptly taken?

Answer:

(a.) Yes, immediately before the collision.

(b.) The helm was put hard-a-starboard and the engines were stopped and put full speed astern.

(c.) Yes.

14. (a.) What was the speed of the *Titanic* shortly before and at the moment of the casualty? (b.) Was such speed excessive under the circumstances?

Answer:

(a.) About 22 knots.

(b.) Yes.

15. (a.) What was the nature of the casualty which happened to the *Titanic* at or about 11.45 p.m. on the 14th April last? (b.) In what latitude and longitude did the casualty occur?

Answer:

(a.) A collision with an iceberg which pierced the starboard side of the vessel in several places below the waterline between the forepeak tank and No. 4 boiler room.

(b.) In latitude 41° 46′ N., longitude 50° 14′ W.

16. (a.) What steps were taken immediately on the happening of the casualty? (b.) How long after the casualty was its seriousness

realised by those in charge of the vessel? (c.) What steps were then taken? (d.) What endeavours were made to save the lives of those on board, and to prevent the vessel from sinking?

Answer:

(a.) The 12 watertight doors in the engine and boiler rooms were closed from the bridge, some of the boiler fires were drawn, and the bilge pumps abaft No. 6 boiler room were started.

(b.) About 15 - 20 minutes.

(c.) and (d.) The boats were ordered to be cleared away. The passengers were roused and orders given to get them on deck, and lifebelts were served out. Some of the watertight doors, other than those in the boiler and engine rooms, were closed. Marconigrams were sent out asking for help. Distress signals (rockets) were fired, and attempts were made to call up by Morse a ship whose lights were seen. Eighteen of the boats were swung out and lowered, and the remaining two floated off the ship and were subsequently utilized as rafts.

17. Was proper discipline maintained on board after the casualty occurred?

Answer:

Yes.

18. (a.) What messages for assistance were sent by the *Titanic* after the casualty and, at what times respectively? (b.) What messages were received by her in response and, at what times respectively? (c.) By what vessels were the messages that were sent by the *Titanic* received, and from what vessels did she receive answers? (d.) What vessels other than the *Titanic* sent or received the messages at or shortly after the casualty in connection with such casualty? (e.) What were the vessels that sent or received such messages? (f.) Were any vessels prevented from going to the assistance of the *Titanic* or her boats owing to messages received from the *Titanic* or owing to any erroneous messages being sent or received? (g.) In regard to such erroneous messages, from what vessels were they sent and by what vessels were they received and at what times respectively?

Answer:

(a.) (b.) (c.) (d.) and (e.) are answered together.

(f.) Several vessels did not go owing to their distance.

(g.) There were no erroneous messages.

(Submitted - Wireless messages in connection with *Titanic* sent the evening of April 14-15, 1912.)

19. (a.) Was the apparatus for lowering the boats on the *Titanic* at the time of the casualty in good working order? (b.) Were the boats swung out, filled, lowered, or otherwise put into the water and got away under proper superintendence? (c.) Were the boats sent away in seaworthy condition and properly manned, equipped and provisioned? (d.) Did the boats, whether those under davits or otherwise, prove to be efficient and serviceable for the purpose of saving life?

Answer:

(a.) Yes.

(b.) Yes.

(c.) The fourteen lifeboats, two emergency boats, and C and D collapsible boats were sent away in a seaworthy condition, but some of them were possibly undermanned. The evidence on this point was unsatisfactory. The total number of crew taken on board the *Carpathia* exceeded the number which would be required for manning the boats. The collapsible boats A and B appeared to have floated off the ship at the time she foundered. The necessary equipment and provisions for the boats were carried in the ship, but some of the boats, nevertheless, left without having their full equipment in them.

(d.) Yes.

20. (a.) What was the number of (a) passengers, (b) crew taken away in each boat on leaving the vessel? (b.) How was this number made up, having regard to: -

1 Sex.

2 Class.

3 Rating.

(c.) How many were children and how many adults? (d.) Did each boat carry its full load and, if not, why not?

Answer:

(a.) (b.) (c.) It is impossible exactly to say how many persons were carried in each boat or what was their sex, class and rating, as the totals given evidence do not correspond with the numbers taken on board the *Carpathia*.

(d.) No.

At least 8 boats did not carry their full loads for the following reasons:

1. Many people did not realise the danger or care to leave the ship at first.

2. Some boats were ordered to be lowered with an idea of then coming round to the gangway doors to complete loading.

3. The officers were not certain of the strength and capacity of the boats in all cases (and see Testimony Re Buckling.).

21. (a.) How many persons on board the *Titanic* at the time of the casualty were ultimately rescued and by what means? (b.) How many lost their lives prior to the arrival of the SS. *Carpathia* in New York? (c.) What was the number of passengers, distinguishing between men and women and adults and children of the 1st, 2nd, and 3rd classes respectively who were saved? (d.) What was the number of the crew, discriminating their ratings and sex, that were saved? (e.) What is the proportion which each of these numbers bears to the corresponding total number on board immediately before the casualty? (f.) What reason is there for the disproportion, if any?

Answer:

(a.) 712, rescued by *Carpathia* from the boats.

(b.) One.

(c.) (d.) and (e.) are answered together.

(f.) The disproportion between the numbers of the passengers saved in the first, second, and third classes is due to various causes, among which the difference in the position of their quarters and the fact that many of the third class passengers were foreigners, are perhaps the most important. Of the Irish emigrants in the third class a large proportion was saved. The disproportion was certainly not due to any discrimination by the officers or crew in assisting the passengers to the boats. The disproportion between the numbers of the passengers and crew saved is due to the fact that the crew, for the most part, all attended to their duties to the last, and until all the boats were gone.

22. What happened to the vessel from the happening of the casualty until she foundered?

Answer:

A detailed description has already been given (see "Description of Damage")

23. Where and at what time did the *Titanic* founder?

Answer:

2.20 a.m. (ship's time) 15th April.

Latitude 41° 46' N., 50° 14' W.

24. (a.) What was the cause of the loss of the *Titanic*, and of the loss of life which thereby ensued or occurred? (b.) What vessels had the opportunity of rendering assistance to the *Titanic* and, if any, how was it that assistance did not reach the *Titanic* before the SS. *Carpathia* arrived? (c.) Was the construction of the vessel and its arrangements such as to make it difficult for any class of passenger or any portion of the crew to take full advantage of any the existing provisions for safety?

Answer:

(a.) Collision with an iceberg and the subsequent foundering of the ship.

(b.) The *Californian*. She could have reached the *Titanic* if she had made the attempt when she saw the first rocket. She made no attempt.

(c.) No.

25. When the *Titanic* left Queenstown on or about 11th April last was she properly constructed and adequately equipped as a passenger steamer and emigrant ship for the Atlantic service?

Answer:

Yes.

26. The Court is invited to report upon the Rules and Regulations made under the Merchant Shipping Acts, 1894 -1906, and the administration of those Acts and of such Rules and Regulations, so far as the consideration thereof is material to this casualty, and to make any recommendations or suggestions that it may think fit, having regard to the circumstances of the casualty, with a view to promoting the safety of vessels and persons at sea.

Answer:

An account of the Board of Trade's Administration has already been given and certain recommendations are subsequently made.

Recommendations

The following recommendations are made. They referred to foreign-going passenger and emigrant steamships.

Watertight Subdivision.

1. That the newly appointed Bulkhead Committee should enquire and report, among other matters, on the desirability and practicability of providing ships with (a.) a double skin carried up above the waterline; or, as an alternative, with (b.) a longitudinal, vertical, watertight bulkhead on each side of the ship, extending as far forward and as far aft as convenient; or (c.) with a combination of (a.) and (b.). Any one of the three (a.), (b.) and (c.) to be in addition to watertight transverse bulkheads.

2. That the Committee should also enquire and report as to the desirability and practicability of fitting ships with (a.) a deck or decks at a convenient distance or distances above the waterline which shall be watertight throughout a part or the whole of the ship's length; and should in this connection report upon (b.) the means by which the

necessary openings in such deck or decks should be made watertight, whether by watertight doors or watertight trunks or by any other and what means.

3. That the Committee should consider and report generally on the practicability of increasing the protection given by subdivision; the object being to secure that the ship shall remain afloat with the greatest practicable proportion of her length in free communication with the sea.

4. That when the Committee has reported upon the matters before mentioned, the Board of Trade should take the report into their consideration and to the extent to which they approve of it should seek Statutory powers to enforce it in all newly built ships, but with a discretion to relax the requirements in special cases where it may seem right to them to do so.

5. That the Board of Trade should be empowered by the Legislature to require the production of the designs and specifications of all ships in their early stages of construction and to direct such amendments of the same as may be thought necessary and practicable for the safety of life at sea in ships. (This should apply to all passenger carrying ships.)

Lifeboats and Rafts.

6. That the provision of lifeboat and raft accommodation on board such ships should be based on the number of persons intended to be carried in the ship and not upon tonnage.

7. That the question of such accommodation should be treated independently of the question of the subdivision of the ship into watertight compartments. (This involves the abolition of Rule 12 of the Life-Saving Appliances Rules of 1902.)

8. That the accommodation should be sufficient for all persons on board, with, however, the qualification that in special cases where, in the opinion Board of Trade, such provision is impracticable, the requirements may be modified as the Board may think right. (In order to give effect to this recommendation changes may be necessary in the sizes and types of boats to be carried and in the method of stowing and floating them. It may also be necessary to set apart one or more of the boat decks exclusively for carrying boats and drilling the crew,

and to consider the distribution of decks in relation to the passengers' quarters. These, however, are matters of detail to be settled with reference to the particular circumstance affecting the ship).

9. That all boats should be fitted with a protective, continuous fender, to lessen the risk of damage when being lowered in a seaway.

10. That the Board of Trade should be empowered to direct that one or more of the boats be fitted with some form of mechanical propulsion.

11. That there should be a Board of Trade regulation requiring all boat equipment (under sections 5 and 6, page 15 of the Rules, dated February, 1902, made by the Board of Trade under section 427, Merchant Shipping Act, 1894) to be in the boats as soon as the ship leaves harbour. The sections quoted above should be amended so as to provide also that all boats and rafts should carry lamps and pyrotechnic lights for purposes of signalling. All boats should be provided with compasses and provisions, and should be very distinctly marked in such a way as to indicate plainly the number of adult persons each boat can carry when being lowered.

12. That the Board of Trade inspection of boats and life-saving appliances should be of a more searching character than hitherto.

Manning the Boats and Boat Drills.

13. That in cases where the deck hands are not sufficient to man the boats enough other members of the crew should be men trained in boat work to make up the deficiency. These men should be required to pass a test in boat work.

14. That in view of the necessity of having on board men trained in boat work, steps should be taken to encourage the training of boys for the Merchant Service.

15. That the operation of Section 115 and Section 134 (a) of the Merchant Shipping Act, 1894, should be examined, with a view to amending the same so as to secure greater continuity of service than hitherto.

16. That the men who are to man the boats should have more frequent drills than hitherto. That in all ships a boat drill, a fire drill and a watertight door drill should be held as soon as possible after leaving the original port of departure and at convenient intervals of

not less than once a week during the voyage. Such drills to be recorded in the official log.

17. That the Board of Trade should be satisfied in each case before the ship leaves port that a scheme has been devised and communicated to each officer of the ship for securing an efficient working of the boats.

General.

18. That every man taking a look-out in such ships should undergo a site test at reasonable intervals.

19. That in all such ships a police system should be organised so as to secure obedience to orders, and proper control and guidance of all on board in times of emergency.

20. That all such ships there should be an installation of wireless telegraphy, and that such installation should be worked with a sufficient number of trained operators to secure a continuous service by night and day. In this connection regard should be had to the resolutions of the International Conference on Wireless Telegraphy recently held under the presidency of Sir H. Babington Smith. That where practicable a silent chamber for "receiving" messages should form part of the installation.

21. That instruction should begin in all Steamship Companies' Regulations that when ice is reported in or near the track the ship should proceed in the dark hours at a moderate speed or alter her course so as to go well clear of the danger zone.

22. That the attention of Masters of vessels should be drawn by the Board of Trade to the effect that under the Maritime Conventions Act, 1911, it is a misdemeanour not to go to the relief of a vessel in distress when possible to do so.

23. That the same protection as to the safety of life in the event of casualties which is afforded to emigrant ships by means of supervision and inspection should be extended to all foreign-going passenger ships.

24. That (unless already done) steps should be taken to call an International Conference to consider and as far as possible to agree upon a common line of conduct in respect of (a) the subdivision of ships; (b) the provision and working of life-saving appliances; (c) the installation of wireless telegraphy and the method of working the

same; (d) the reduction of speed or the alteration of course in the vicinity of ice; and (e) the use of searchlights.

MERSEY.
Wreck Commissioner

We concur,
ARTHUR GOUGH-CALTHORPE,
A. W. CLARKE,
F. C. A. LYON,
J. H. BILES,
EDWARD C. CHASTON.
Assessors.
30th July, 1912.

www.ingramcontent.com/pod-product-compliance
Lightning Source LLC
LaVergne TN
LVHW051121080426
835510LV00018B/2170